OUTDOOR LIFE LISTS

A List-by-List Guide to Enjoying the Great Outdoors

BARBARA ANN KIPFER

FALCON®

ESSEX, CONNECTICUT

An imprint of Globe Pequot, the trade division of The Rowman & Littlefield Publishing Group, Inc.
4501 Forbes Blvd., Ste. 200
Lanham, MD 20706
www.rowman.com

Falcon and FalconGuides are registered trademarks and Make Adventure Your Story is a trademark of The Rowman & Littlefield Publishing Group, Inc.

Distributed by NATIONAL BOOK NETWORK

Illustrations ©:
appleuzr/DigitalVision Vectors via Getty Images
rambo182/iStock/Getty Images Plus
LueratSatichob/DigitalVision Vectors via Getty Images
vreemous/DigitalVision Vectors via Getty Images
Rakdee/DigitalVision Vectors via Getty Images
BestVectorStock/iStock/Getty Images Plus
mystockicons/DigitalVision Vectors via Getty Images

British Library Cataloguing in Publication Information available

Library of Congress Cataloging-in-Publication Data

Names: Kipfer, Barbara Ann, author.
Title: Outdoor life lists : a list-by-list guide to enjoying the great
    outdoors / Barbara Ann Kipfer.
Description: Essex, Connecticut : Falcon, [2024] | Includes index.
Identifiers: LCCN 2023041508 (print) | LCCN 2023041509 (ebook) | ISBN
    9781493076680 (paperback) | ISBN 9781493076673 (epub)
Subjects: LCSH: Outdoor recreation—Equipment and supplies. | Sporting goods.
Classification: LCC GV191.623 .K57 2024 (print) | LCC GV191.623 (ebook) |
    DDC 796.5—dc23/eng/20231018
LC record available at https://lccn.loc.gov/2023041508
LC ebook record available at https://lccn.loc.gov/2023041509

∞™ The paper used in this publication meets the minimum requirements of American National Standard for Information Sciences—Permanence of Paper for Printed Library Materials, ANSI/NISO Z39.48-1992.

TO PAUL, MY BOON COMPANION
IN THE GREAT OUTDOORS

(AND INDOORS)

CONTENTS

RECREATION 62

(defined as activities that are not rule-based and may be done as an individual or with others)

ACTIVITIES 136

(defined as being more focused on nature, community or family-oriented)

SAFETY 171

INDEX 206

ABOUT THE AUTHOR 209

INTRODUCTION

Outdoor Life Lists is an informative celebration of the outdoors. Look inside to find seventy-five checklists covering the essentials and potential extras to consider for enjoying outdoor sports, recreation, and activities. These lists cover the things you need to bring and wear to fully and safely participate in every activity. A fourth part of the book contains safety lists.

Accompanying each section is a how-to sidebar in the form of a checklist—such as how to manage chafing, orient a map, or camp in the desert. These how-tos may come in handy in various outdoor situations, so you can also find them using the index.

To top it off, there are sidebars with short lists of things one may observe and be happy about during each of the outdoor activities.

This book is intended to be a general guide for items readers need for the most enjoyable and fulfilling experiences in outdoor activities. It is an entry- and intermediate-level book that identifies outdoor gear that readers should have or consider. The equipment lists are necessarily broad in order to cover the four seasons as well as regional differences.

The lists can be combined for multiple-activity use—for example, a camping trip planned with mountain biking and/or water sports. Since each outdoor enthusiast may have unique needs that are not covered here, space is provided to add to the base checklists.

Outdoor Life Lists offers need-to-know information on how best to commune with Mother Nature, and the sections on first aid, lifesaving, and survival touch all outdoor activities. Becoming familiar with the safety checklists is a responsibility to yourself, to others, and to the environment.

SPORTS

(defined as activities usually with rules, often in teams or as competition)

1. Baseball and Softball
2. Basketball
3. Beach Volleyball
4. Bicycle Racing
5. Bouldering
6. Climbing, Rock
7. Cross-Country Skiing
8. Distance Running, Marathoning
9. Football, Flag/Touch
10. Golf
11. Ice Climbing
12. Ice Hockey
13. Mountaineering
14. Paddleball
15. Pickleball
16. Platform Tennis
17. Rowing
18. Skiing

BASEBALL AND SOFTBALL

Essentials

- ❐ Athletic cup or supporter
- ❐ Ball cap
- ❐ Base layer clothing
- ❐ Baseball bag or duffel
- ❐ Baseball bat
- ❐ Baseball belt
- ❐ Baseball pants
- ❐ Baseball sliding or compression shorts
- ❐ Baseball socks
- ❐ Baseballs
- ❐ Batting glove
- ❐ Batting helmet
- ❐ Cleats
- ❐ Leather or synthetic baseball glove/mitt
- ❐ Mouthguard
- ❐ On-field heart protection shirt
- ❐ Practice shirts
- ❐ Protective gear for playing position and batting (chest, wrist, or leg guards)

Extras

- ❐ Athletic tape
- ❐ Baseball bucket
- ❐ Baseball rebound net
- ❐ Batting tee
- ❐ Compression arm or leg sleeves
- ❐ Eye black
- ❐ First-aid kit
- ❐ Food and snacks
- ❐ Practice balls
- ❐ Rebound net
- ❐ Replacement shoelaces
- ❐ Sports drink
- ❐ Sunglasses
- ❐ Sunscreen and lip balm
- ❐ Swing trainer
- ❐ Training balls
- ❐ Water bottle

Softball

- ❐ Fastpitch bat
- ❐ Softball glove or mitt
- ❐ Softball pants
- ❐ Softballs

DEAL WITH INSECTS

— Wear long-sleeve shirts and long pants that are lightweight and light-colored.
— Dark-colored clothes do not draw as many insects, but darker is hotter and it is harder to see insects on the clothes.
— Tuck pants into socks and shirt into pants. Wear a hat to keep insects off head and hair.
— Consider wearing insect-repellent clothing (Permethrin-treated).
— Use DEET-based insect repellents of 15 to 30 percent solution or an insect repellent of your choice.
— Avoid brush, hanging branches, and tall grasses.
— To avoid bees, yellow jackets, and other stinging insects, try not to look or smell like a flower. Swatting or rapid movement is not helpful and may provoke an attack.

THINGS TO BE HAPPY ABOUT OUTDOORS

- shadows and cloud formations
- a butterfly landing on you
- inhaling the scents of the season
- the ruckus of birdsong
- sunshine replacing the clouds

BASKETBALL

Essentials

- ❏ Ball pump and needle
- ❏ Basketball(s)
- ❏ Basketball bag or duffel
- ❏ Basketball shoes
- ❏ Basketball socks
- ❏ First-aid kit
- ❏ Mouthguard
- ❏ T-shirts, jerseys, shorts
- ❏ Warmup suit or jacket
- ❏ Water bottle

Extras

- ❏ Compression shorts
- ❏ Headband
- ❏ Jumper knee straps
- ❏ Leg sleeves or knee pads
- ❏ Practice basketball

THINGS TO BE HAPPY ABOUT OUTDOORS

- ivy growing on brick walls
- sky perfectly blue
- the soft light of early evening
- shadows of birds flying overhead
- a flower unfolding

DEFEND AGAINST A COYOTE

— Scare the coyote with loud noises and by making yourself look large.
— Yank the tail to free a child or animal from the coyote.
— Kick the coyote in the ribs.
— Move to high ground if possible.

❒ Practice basketball shoes

❒ Practice basketball shorts

❒ Shooter sleeve

❒ Slides (shoes for locker room)

❒ Sports bra

❒ Sports drink, snacks, food

❒ Wristband

BEACH VOLLEYBALL

Essentials

❑ Beach towel

❑ Extra swimsuit

❑ Hat or visor

❑ Lip balm

❑ Snacks and beverages

❑ Sunglasses

❑ Sunscreen

❑ Sweatshirt or windbreaker

❑ Swimsuit

❑ Volleyball

❑ Water bottle

Extras

❑ Camp shoes or sandals

❑ Knee pads or knee straps

❑ Net and boundary markers

❑ Palm protectors

❑ Sand socks

THINGS TO BE HAPPY ABOUT OUTDOORS

- driftwood, worn satin-smooth
- savoring unadulterated waters
- a butterfly coming straight at you
- the whorls of a shell
- gulls riding the breeze

STAY COOL OR COOL OFF

- Avoid the hottest part of the day, usually between noon and 3 p.m.
- If you can, do your activity in an area that offers shade from trees, stone walls, and so on.
- Or, if you can, do your activity near a body of water, which often provides a breeze. You can also cool off with the water.
- Wear light colors that reflect the sun's rays. The fabric should be lightweight, loose-fitting, possibly vented, and moisture-wicking. Consider UPF-rated clothing for more sun protection.
- Wear a hat with a fuller brim. Try using a headband or wristband(s) to wipe your face.
- Use a bandanna, handkerchief, or neck gaiter (buff) for neck moisture. These can be wetted to make you cooler. Specially designed "'cooling" neck cloths are also available.
- Water is key, so carry a water bottle, hydration pack, extra water, and perhaps a squirt/mist bottle of water.

BICYCLE RACING

Essentials

- ❐ Bike
- ❐ Cell phone
- ❐ Clothes for after the race
- ❐ Cycling multi-tool with Allen wrenches
- ❐ Cycling shoes
- ❐ Driver's license, medical info, emergency contact card
- ❐ Extra water or sports drink
- ❐ Eye protection or sunglasses
- ❐ First-aid kit
- ❐ Food and snacks
- ❐ Gloves, padded (fingerless for warm weather, full-fingered for cool)

- ❐ Helmet
- ❐ Ibuprofen, aspirin, or other pain reliever
- ❐ Jersey, wicking
- ❐ Lip balm
- ❐ Membership card (if applicable)
- ❐ Money, cash, or check
- ❐ Padded shorts
- ❐ Patch kit and/or spare tube(s)
- ❐ Pump
- ❐ Race flyer and directions
- ❐ Racing license or rider release printout from website

PRE-BIKING CHECKLIST

- — Tire pressure and condition
- — Seat and handlebar height
- — Brakes
- — Lights and reflectors
- — Lubrication
- — Bolt tightness
- — Quick-release secured (if bike is so equipped)

THINGS TO BE HAPPY ABOUT OUTDOORS

- patches of tender grass
- the sun's rays shining down through clouds
- wind at your back
- plants growing in straight rows
- wildflowers

❒ Safety pins for your race number

❒ Socks (tall or thermal socks for cool weather)

❒ Sunscreen

❒ Tire levers

❒ Towels

❒ Underlayer in cool weather

❒ Watch or cycling computer

❒ Water bottle(s)

❒ Weather-resistant shell

❒ Wet wipes

Extras

❒ Antacids

❒ Backpack

❒ Camera

❒ Lock

❒ Map

❒ Prescription medications

❒ Saddle (underseat) bag

❒ Tights

❒ Toilet paper

BOULDERING

Essentials

- ❏ Appropriate clothing
- ❏ Ascender
- ❏ Backpack
- ❏ Bouldering crash pads or mat
- ❏ Brush(es) including hold brush
- ❏ Chalk and chalk bag
- ❏ Climbing shoes
- ❏ Finger tape
- ❏ Headlamp
- ❏ Helmet
- ❏ Insulation layer
- ❏ Jacket
- ❏ Rope
- ❏ Skin care kit
- ❏ Snacks
- ❏ Water

THINGS TO BE HAPPY ABOUT OUTDOORS

- the white and gray of granite peaks
- rock walls at dawn
- patterns in nature
- phantom rain in a desert
- hawks and falcons soaring by

SET UP A SHADE SHELTER

— Find a natural dip in the land.
— Dig a space for your body.
— Stretch a blanket over the hole.
— Anchor the blanket with rocks.

Extras

- ❏ Approach shoes
- ❏ Belay device
- ❏ Carabiners
- ❏ Climbing cams
- ❏ Climbing harness
- ❏ Climbing protection
- ❏ Crampons
- ❏ Guidebook or map
- ❏ Ice tool
- ❏ Hexes
- ❏ Quickdraws
- ❏ Sling

CLIMBING, ROCK

Essentials

- ❏ Approach shoes
- ❏ Backpack
- ❏ Bandanna or buff
- ❏ Belay/rappel device
- ❏ Binoculars
- ❏ Carabiners, locking and nonlocking
- ❏ Cell phone in protective bag
- ❏ Chalk and chalk bag
- ❏ Energy snacks and beverages
- ❏ Finger tape
- ❏ First-aid kit
- ❏ Food
- ❏ Hand protection: belay/rappel gloves or tape
- ❏ Harness
- ❏ Hat
- ❏ Headlamp or flashlight and extra batteries
- ❏ Helmet
- ❏ Insect repellent
- ❏ Insulation: jacket, vest, other layers
- ❏ Knife or multi-tool
- ❏ Multifunction watch
- ❏ Notepad and pen or pencil
- ❏ Permits

CAMP IN THE DESERT

- — Keep your distance from wildlife.
- — Camp on high ground, but avoid dangerous exposed ridges or peaks.
- — Pitch the tent facing away from the east to avoid a sunrise awakening.
- — Secure tent lines to steel rods, then top with plastic bottles to protect feet and ankles.
- — Shake out your shoes before putting them on.
- — Bring and drink 1 gallon of water per person per day.

- ❒ Quickdraws
- ❒ Rainwear
- ❒ Rock climbing shoes
- ❒ Rope
- ❒ Route description or guidebook
- ❒ Runners, singles and doubles

- ❒ Shorts, pants, top
- ❒ Signaling mirror
- ❒ Sunglasses and retainer strap
- ❒ Sunscreen
- ❒ Water bottle(s)

Extras

- ❒ Camera
- ❒ Duffel
- ❒ Emergency reflective blanket
- ❒ Hand sanitizer
- ❒ Lip balm
- ❒ Rope bag

- ❒ Sanitation trowel
- ❒ Socks
- ❒ Toilet paper
- ❒ Trash bag
- ❒ Two-way radios
- ❒ Water treatment method
- ❒ Wicking T-shirt

CROSS-COUNTRY SKIING

Essentials

- ❐ Active winter clothing: base layer, mid-layer, outer layer, and extra clothes
- ❐ Boots
- ❐ Cell phone
- ❐ Daypack or backpack
- ❐ Eye protection or sunglasses
- ❐ Fire: matches or lighter
- ❐ First aid
- ❐ Food and extra food
- ❐ Gloves or mittens
- ❐ Hand and toe warmers
- ❐ Hat or balaclava

GO TO THE BATHROOM IN THE WOODS

- — Follow Leave No Trace principles. Check the regulations in the area you plan to visit.
- — Stay 200 feet (about seventy steps) away from the trail, campsites, and water sources.
- — Choose a brushy area for privacy if you like.
- — Find a soft spot of earth. Watch the slope so that pee runs away from you.
- — Dig a cat hole about 4 inches wide and 6 to 8 inches deep with a stick, rock, boot heel, or trowel.
- — Take a wide stance and make sure clothes, boot laces, and straps are out of the way.
- — Fill the cat hole with the original dirt and place a rock or branch over or upright to discourage it being dug up.
- — If you use toilet paper or tissue, put in a resealable zipper bag. Pack it out with you.
- — Use hand sanitizer or wipes afterward.

- ❏ Headlamp and extra batteries
- ❏ Knife and gear repair kit
- ❏ Navigation: compass, map, GPS, altimeter, personal locator beacon and/or satellite messenger
- ❏ Neck gaiter (buff)
- ❏ Poles and straps
- ❏ Shelter (emergency)
- ❏ Skis
- ❏ Spare gloves and socks
- ❏ Sun protection
- ❏ Vacuum bottle with hot liquids
- ❏ Water and extra water
- ❏ Waxing gear: scraper, paste or rub-on wax, kick wax, cork

Extras

- ❏ Cross-country ski belt
- ❏ Duct tape
- ❏ Electric gloves and insoles
- ❏ Emergency blanket
- ❏ Gaiters
- ❏ Headband
- ❏ Ski pass
- ❏ Watch and heart rate monitor
- ❏ Whistle

DISTANCE RUNNING, MARATHONING

Essentials

- ❏ Anti-chafing products
- ❏ Backpack or duffel
- ❏ Bib number and safety pins
- ❏ Cell phone
- ❏ Course map
- ❏ Extra shirt and shorts/pants
- ❏ Extra socks
- ❏ First-aid kit
- ❏ Food and beverages for during and after the race
- ❏ Hat or visor
- ❏ ID
- ❏ Lip balm
- ❏ Pain relievers
- ❏ Race entry information: race confirmation, location, bib number pick-up
- ❏ Raincoat or poncho for staying dry before the start

THINGS TO BE HAPPY ABOUT OUTDOORS

- a silhouette of a dandelion
- the seasonal feeling of the air
- brown, old earth
- deer on a hillside
- a starling murmuration

STAY ON TRACK IN THE DESERT

— Dunes are often crescent-shaped.
— The "points" of the crescent will tell you which way is downwind.
— Use this information to stay on track as you hike in the desert.

❒ Running clothes

❒ Running shoes

❒ Socks

❒ Sunscreen

❒ Towel

❒ Warm top and bottom for before and after the race

❒ Watch or GPS

❒ Water bottle

❒ Waterproof jacket

Extras

❒ Gloves

❒ Massage oil

❒ Money

❒ Orthotics if necessary

❒ Prescription medication

❒ Running tights

❒ Sunglasses

❒ Timing chip

❒ Tissues

❒ Toilet paper

FOOTBALL, FLAG/TOUCH

Essentials

- ❏ Cones
- ❏ Duffel bag or backpack
- ❏ First-aid kit
- ❏ Flag football belts
- ❏ Flag football shorts
- ❏ Flag football spotter
- ❏ Flags
- ❏ Food and drink
- ❏ Football
- ❏ Football cleats
- ❏ Football socks
- ❏ Jerseys (two colors)
- ❏ Mouthguard
- ❏ Receiver gloves
- ❏ Supporter (athletic cup, etc.) or sports bra
- ❏ Towel
- ❏ Water bottle

Extras

- ❏ Compression apparel
- ❏ Hand warmers

THINGS TO BE HAPPY ABOUT OUTDOORS

- pigs in clover
- a snowman on the field
- the prolate spheroid shape of the ball
- the call of an eagle or hawk
- the last rays of sunlight

LEAVE NO TRACE PRINCIPLES

— Plan ahead and prepare.
— Travel and camp on durable surfaces.
— Dispose of waste properly.
— Minimize campfire impacts.
— Leave what you find.
— Respect wildlife.
— Be considerate of others.

GOLF

Essentials

- ❑ Ball marker
- ❑ Cell phone
- ❑ Club brush
- ❑ Divot repair tool
- ❑ Food and snacks
- ❑ Golf bag
- ❑ Golf balls
- ❑ Golf club covers
- ❑ Golf clubs: driver, woods, irons, wedges, hybrids, putter
- ❑ Golf gloves
- ❑ Golf shoes
- ❑ Golf towel
- ❑ Hat, cap, or visor
- ❑ Insect repellent
- ❑ Practice balls
- ❑ Sunglasses
- ❑ Sunscreen
- ❑ Tees
- ❑ Umbrella or rain hood
- ❑ Watch or GPS
- ❑ Water bottle

Extras

- ❑ Ball retriever
- ❑ Ball washer

☐ Golf cart

☐ Heavy drive or weighted donut

☐ Lead tape

☐ Positional guides

☐ Rangefinder

☐ Stroke counter

☐ Swing trainer

READ STORM CLOUDS

— Cumulonimbus are fierce storm clouds, recognizable by their distinctive anvil shape.
— Cumulus are small, lumpy clouds; rising hot air can turn them into thundering cumulonimbus.
— Nimbostratus bring rain, snow, and danger; these ragged-bottom clouds are an ominous gray.
— Stratocumulus form close-together lumpy rows; a change in air density can turn them into stormy nimbostratus.

ICE CLIMBING

Essentials

- ❏ Backpack
- ❏ Belay device
- ❏ Belay jacket
- ❏ Climbing harness
- ❏ Emergency blanket
- ❏ Food and water
- ❏ Gloves
- ❏ Hand warmers
- ❏ Headlamp
- ❏ Helmet
- ❏ Ice axes
- ❏ Ice climbing crampons

TIE A BASIC KNOT

— For the bowline knot or bowline hitch: Lay the rope down on a flat surface. Hold the right end of the rope in your hand and create a loop a little less than halfway down the string by placing the right end over the center.

— Pull the right end of the rope through the loop. The right-hand end should come toward you as it goes through the loop. Don't pull the knot taut yet.

— Bring the left end of the rope up and tuck the right end behind it. This will create a smaller top loop above the large loop you already made.

— Pull the right end back through the top loop. Thread it through so that the rope is going away from you instead of toward you.

— Pull the two ends of the rope away from each other to tighten the knot. This leaves you with a knot and a large loop at the end.

THINGS TO BE HAPPY ABOUT OUTDOORS

- wind-polished ice
- the mineral composition of ice
- frozen waterfalls
- deer waiting
- branches groaning

☐ Ice climbing rack supplies: ice screws, holders, quickdraws/alpine draws, slings, locking carabiners, cordelette or webbing, V-thread hook

☐ Ice tools

☐ Knife

☐ Mountaineering boots

☐ Personal safety gear: first-aid kit and medications

☐ Proper clothing: base layer, mid-layer, outer layer

☐ Rope

☐ Safety beacon

☐ Spare sling and carabiners

☐ Sunglasses

Extras

☐ Avalanche safety equipment

☐ Camera

☐ Extra boots

☐ Extra gloves

☐ Portable charger

☐ Toilet paper

ICE HOCKEY

Essentials

- ☐ Base layer
- ☐ Compression shorts
- ☐ Equipment bag
- ☐ Face mask
- ☐ First-aid kit
- ☐ Helmet repair kit
- ☐ Hockey belt/garter
- ☐ Hockey gloves
- ☐ Hockey jersey
- ☐ Hockey pants
- ☐ Hockey skates
- ☐ Hockey socks
- ☐ Hockey stick
- ☐ Hockey suspenders
- ☐ Mouthguard
- ☐ Neck guard
- ☐ Pads: elbow, shoulder, shin
- ☐ Pucks
- ☐ Skate blade guards or soakers
- ☐ Skate laces
- ☐ Skate sharpening tools or kit
- ☐ Skull cap
- ☐ Stick tape or wax
- ☐ Supporter (athletic cup) or sports bra
- ☐ Training pucks or balls
- ☐ Water bottle

THINGS TO BE HAPPY ABOUT OUTDOORS

- snow spread over hills
- the moon rising
- pink clouds
- evergreens' red berries
- fish under frozen water

STAY WARM OR GET WARM

— Choose clothing layers. Add and remove layers to stay warm and comfortable.
— Cover as much skin as possible.
— Nothing should be too tight, as that can cause poor circulation and frostbite.
— If your clothes get wet, change to dry clothes.
— Wear lightweight or shell gloves under gloves or mittens. Have extra gloves with you.
— If your feet get wet, change into the extra socks you brought.
— A winter hat or headband can be accompanied by a neck gaiter (buff) or face mask (balaclava).
— Consider packing a vacuum-insulated bottle with a hot beverage.
— Consider packing hand and foot warmers.
— Never stay out in the cold if it is unbearable or scary. Just turn back and go home.

Extras

❐ Emergency blanket

❐ Face mask defogger

❐ Goaltending equipment if you are goalie

❐ Multi-tool

❐ Snacks and food

❐ Sock tape

MOUNTAINEERING

Essentials

❏ Avalanche transceiver

❏ Bandanna or buff

❏ Batteries and extra batteries for devices

❏ Battery pack or solar panel

❏ Belay/rappel device

❏ Boots (crampon-compatible)

❏ Carabiners, locking and nonlocking

❏ Cell phone

❏ Climbing pack

❏ Compass

❏ Crampons

❏ Crevasse rescue gear: snow picket, slings, lightweight pulleys, accessory cords

❏ Duct tape

❏ Emergency shelter

❏ Firestarter, lighter, matches in waterproof container

❏ First-aid kit

❏ Fleece and insulating jacket or vest

❏ Food and drinks, extra supply of food (in bearproof container)

❏ Gloves or mittens or other hand protection

❏ GPS and altimeter watch

❏ Harness

❏ Hats, insulating, sun-shielding

❏ Headlamp or flashlight plus spare

THINGS TO BE HAPPY ABOUT OUTDOORS

- flat rock
- a full moon blazing
- nature in a white sleep
- a geological layer cake
- soft beds of fresh pine needles

❏ Helmet

❏ Ice axe with leash

❏ ID and car keys

❏ Itinerary left with friend and also under car seat

❏ Kitchen gear and stove

❏ Knife or multi-tool

❏ Lip balm

❏ Long underwear

❏ Map with protective case

❏ Pants, top for mountaineering, wicking base layers

❏ Permits

❏ Personal hygiene kit

❏ Probe

❏ Prusik cords

❏ Pulley

❏ Rainwear

❏ Rope

❏ Route description or guidebook

❏ Runners, singles and doubles

AVOID LIGHTNING ON A MOUNTAIN

— Separate yourself from other people.
— Remove metal and jewelry from body.
— Walk down to a lower position and avoid trees.
— Put down an insulating layer if possible.
— Crouch with hands off the ground and mouth open.

❏ Satellite messenger and/or personal locator beacon

❏ Shovel

❏ Signaling mirror

❏ Sleeping bag and pads

❏ Snow climbing protection gear

❏ Socks plus spares

❏ Sunglasses or goggles

❏ Sunscreen

❏ Tent, tarp, reflective blanket

❏ Towel and biodegradable soap

❏ Water bottles and/or hydration system

❏ Water treatment system

❏ Waterproof container

❏ Whistle

Extras

❏ Binoculars

❏ Blister treatment supplies

❏ Camming devices

- ❏ Gaiters
- ❏ Hand warmers
- ❏ Hexes
- ❏ Ice screws
- ❏ Ice tools with leashes
- ❏ Insect repellent
- ❏ Insulated sit pad
- ❏ Journal and pen or pencil
- ❏ Money
- ❏ Nose guard
- ❏ Nut extraction tool
- ❏ Nuts
- ❏ Reading material or games
- ❏ Two-way radios
- ❏ Urination products
- ❏ Wands

PADDLEBALL

Essentials

- ❏ First-aid kit
- ❏ Glove
- ❏ Goggles
- ❏ Paddle bag
- ❏ Paddleball balls
- ❏ Paddleball racket
- ❏ Snacks
- ❏ Sneakers
- ❏ Towel
- ❏ Water

Extras

- ❏ Ball hopper
- ❏ Braces or supports
- ❏ Eye protection or sunglasses
- ❏ Grip tape
- ❏ Hat
- ❏ ID and keys
- ❏ Paddle cover
- ❏ Portable net

THINGS TO BE HAPPY ABOUT OUTDOORS

- a small tree, growing
- squirrels with the bushiest tails
- the sky changing color
- a birdwatchers' path
- earth laughing in flowers

RECOGNIZE POISONOUS PLANTS

— The old saying of "Leaves of three, let it be!" is a helpful reminder for identifying poison ivy and poison oak. That does not apply to poison sumac, however, which usually has clusters of seven to thirteen leaves. And even poison ivy and poison oak may have more than three leaf clusters, depending on the environment and season. You would be smart to familiarize yourself with what these plants look like in different seasons.

— Eastern poison ivy and oak are typically hairy, ropelike vines with three shiny green leaves budding from one small stem. The leaves may be red in the fall.

— Western poison ivy is typically a low shrub with three leaves that does not form a climbing vine. Pacific poison oak may be vine-like.

— Stinging nettle is known for its brightly colored, yellow or pink flowers, which poison ivy, oak, and sumac are not.

— The best way to identify poisonous plants is to become familiar with pictures of varieties growing in the area. This is because poisonous plants come in so many forms that any rule of thumb will not be sufficient.

— Besides the saying, "Leaves of three, let it be!" there is also the saying, "Alternate is not great." These plants often have leaf stems that alternate on the branch; they are not directly opposite each other. Even the veins on the leaflets alternate and are never directly opposite. And any flowers growing on these plants alternate on the branches and are not directly opposite each other.

— You can also carry a printed guide (or app) for identifying plants.

PICKLEBALL

Essentials

- ❐ First-aid kit
- ❐ Glove
- ❐ Paddle bag
- ❐ Pickleball balls
- ❐ Pickleball paddle
- ❐ Snacks
- ❐ Sneakers
- ❐ Towel
- ❐ Water

Extras

- ❐ Braces or supports
- ❐ Eye protection or sunglasses
- ❐ Grip tape
- ❐ Hat
- ❐ ID and keys
- ❐ Paddle cover
- ❐ Portable net

THINGS TO BE HAPPY ABOUT OUTDOORS

- sunlight silhouetting tree trunks
- a cobweb trembling at sunrise
- birds' mating calls
- a raccoon peering out
- ladybug spots

MANAGE STRESS

— Virtually any form of physical activity can act as a stress reliever. Doing a sport, recreation, or activity outdoors is even better.

— Look at your time outdoors as medicine. The plants, trees, and oxygen are calming.

— Contemplate natural scenes. Don't just pass by something impressive; pause and take it in fully.

— Disconnect from your phone while you are outdoors. The phone can be a helpful tool with its many functions. But leave it at that. Don't focus on taking photos for your social media.

— Slow down and stop often. Don't be in a hurry to get through your outdoor activity.

— Take long, deep breaths whenever you can.

— Engage all your senses. Listen to and look at the trees, animals, birds, and insects. Touch and feel natural articles.

— When you stop, be still.

PLATFORM TENNIS

Essentials

- ❏ First-aid kit
- ❏ Glove
- ❏ Goggles
- ❏ Paddle bag
- ❏ Platform tennis balls
- ❏ Platform tennis racket
- ❏ Snacks
- ❏ Sneakers
- ❏ Towel
- ❏ Water

Extras

- ❏ Ball hopper
- ❏ Braces or supports
- ❏ Eye protection or sunglasses
- ❏ Grip tape
- ❏ Hat
- ❏ ID and keys
- ❏ Paddle cover
- ❏ Portable net

PROTECT ANIMAL COMPANIONS

— Make sure your pet is physically ready to be part of your outdoor activity. Factor in age, size, immune system, vaccine schedule, and so on.
— Make sure your pet has the vaccinations and preventive medicines needed for the outdoor destination.
— Know the regulations for the area where you will be. Some parks and trails do not allow pets. Leashes are mandatory almost everywhere.
— Hydration is very important. Carry fresh water and have a collapsible dish if needed. Do not let the pet drink untreated water.
— Consider bringing a pet towel, cooling collar, insect repellent collar, nail clippers, and a safety light to clip on your pet.
— Watch to make sure your pet is not overdoing it. Heatstroke is a possibility.
— If your dog cannot swim, pack a dog PFD. Even a good swimmer will need help in whitewater. And lakes get very cool, so be careful about a dog swimming in one.
— Keep pets away for wildlife, and halt chewing immediately if they gnaw on a plant.
— Always check for ticks.

THINGS TO BE HAPPY ABOUT OUTDOORS

- a bird taking a bath
- pine cones opening
- zigzagging animal tracks
- rows of vines
- sun washing the earth

ROWING

Essentials

- ❐ Boat
- ❐ First-aid kit
- ❐ Gloves
- ❐ Goggles
- ❐ Hat
- ❐ Life jacket or personal flotation device (PDF)
- ❐ Paddle/oar
- ❐ Proper clothing for weather, especially layers
- ❐ Rainwear
- ❐ Snacks
- ❐ Sunglasses
- ❐ Sunscreen
- ❐ Towel
- ❐ Water bottle
- ❐ Water shoes

Extras

- ❐ Megaphone
- ❐ Oar cover
- ❐ Plastic bags
- ❐ Socks
- ❐ Tights
- ❐ Transportation trailer
- ❐ Visor

THINGS TO BE HAPPY ABOUT OUTDOORS

- a seashell whispering in your ear
- pebbles of sea glass
- fresh harbor wind
- no traffic sounds
- the varied colors of the water

DETERMINE DISTANCE TRAVELED

— You can use a smartwatch or phone with a fitness app to determine how much distance you have traveled.
— Pace length is not as accurate as a fitness app or GPS, but it gives a reasonable approximation of distance traveled. First, measure your stride. A pace or complete stride is a measured two steps. Two steps are likely about 50 to 60 inches.
— You can figure a pace average on a controlled course before using the method to measure the distance on a walk or hike. You can use a football field or track for this.
— You can use a map and compass or a pedometer or pedometer phone app.

SKIING

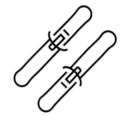

Essentials

- ❏ Backpack or daypack
- ❏ Balaclava or buff
- ❏ Base and mid-layers
- ❏ Batteries and extra batteries for devices
- ❏ Bindings
- ❏ Cell phone
- ❏ First-aid kit
- ❏ Food, snacks, beverages
- ❏ Foot warmers
- ❏ Gloves or mittens
- ❏ GPS or personal locator beacon
- ❏ Hand warmers
- ❏ Lift ticket or pass
- ❏ Lip balm
- ❏ Long underwear
- ❏ Neck warmer
- ❏ Signaling mirror
- ❏ Ski boot bag or backpack
- ❏ Ski boots
- ❏ Ski goggles
- ❏ Ski helmet
- ❏ Ski jacket
- ❏ Ski snow pants
- ❏ Ski poles
- ❏ Ski socks (wool)
- ❏ Skis
- ❏ Sunglasses
- ❏ Sunscreen
- ❏ Trail map

THINGS TO BE HAPPY ABOUT OUTDOORS

- sounds that snow and ice make
- woodsmoke on the wind
- sunlight slanting through trees
- things that happen at dusk or twilight
- sunshine and freedom

- ☐ Water bottle or hydration pack
- ☐ Whistle
- ☐ Winter hat

Extras

- ☐ Aprés-ski clothes
- ☐ Avalanche kit
- ☐ Camp shoes or slides
- ☐ Compression socks
- ☐ Ear warmer
- ☐ Go Pro helmet camera
- ☐ Heated gloves
- ☐ Knee guards
- ☐ Portable charger
- ☐ Ski car rack
- ☐ Ski tuning equipment
- ☐ Slope meter
- ☐ Snow boots

LAYER CLOTHING

— Know yourself in regard to body temperature and heat. Do you feel really warm or cold in certain circumstances?

— Start with a base layer (underwear, T-shirt) that is wicking (polyester, nylon, other synthetics, wool). It needs to keep you cool when it is warm and prevent you from getting chilled or hypothermic when it is cold.

— The mid-layer is for insulation to retain body heat to keep you warm.

— The outer layer is a shell that shields from wind and precipitation.

— Layers are often rated for being lightweight, midweight, or heavyweight or by warmth (e.g., uninsulated, warm, warmer, warmest).

— Layers allow you to adjust your clothing when the weather changes.

SNOWBOARDING

Essentials

- ❏ Backpack or daypack
- ❏ Balaclava or buff
- ❏ Base and mid-layers
- ❏ Batteries and extra batteries for devices
- ❏ Bindings
- ❏ Cell phone
- ❏ First-aid kit
- ❏ Food, snacks, beverages
- ❏ Foot warmers
- ❏ Hand warmers
- ❏ Lift ticket or pass
- ❏ Lip balm
- ❏ Long underwear
- ❏ Neck warmer
- ❏ Signaling mirror
- ❏ Snowboard
- ❏ Snowboard bag
- ❏ Snowboard boots
- ❏ Snowboard gloves
- ❏ Snowboard goggles
- ❏ Snowboard helmet
- ❏ Snowboard jacket
- ❏ Snowboard leash
- ❏ Snowboard lock
- ❏ Snowboard pants
- ❏ Snowboard socks
- ❏ Snowboard wax
- ❏ Sunglasses

THINGS TO BE HAPPY ABOUT OUTDOORS

- snow sculptures
- cranberries or holly berries
- powder snow
- evergreens with beards
- lumbering gray clouds

BUILD A CAMPFIRE

— Make a pile of dry tinder.
— Form a tepee of sticks.
— Surround that with a tepee of larger branches.
— Ignite tinder.

❏ Sunscreen

❏ Trail map

❏ Water bottle or hydration pack

❏ Whistle

❏ Winter hat

Extras

❏ Aprés-ski clothes

❏ Avalanche kit

❏ Board tools

❏ Camp shoes or slides

❏ Compression socks

❏ Ear warmer

❏ Go Pro helmet camera

❏ Heated gloves

❏ Knee guards

❏ Portable charger

❏ Slope meter

❏ Snow boots

❏ Tuning vises

SOCCER

Essentials

- ☐ Ball pump
- ☐ Cold-weather layer
- ☐ Extra shirt, shorts, socks
- ☐ First-aid kit
- ☐ Gear bag
- ☐ Mouthguard
- ☐ Rainwear
- ☐ Shin guard sleeves, tape, straps
- ☐ Shin guards and pads
- ☐ Snacks and food
- ☐ Soccer ball
- ☐ Soccer cleats
- ☐ Soccer socks
- ☐ Sunscreen and lip balm
- ☐ Uniform: shirt, shorts, warmup pants
- ☐ Water bottle

THINGS TO BE HAPPY ABOUT OUTDOORS

- a rainbow
- nature throwing one last party
- stridulation, the noise of crickets
- yellowish fields bathed in cold sunshine
- moonrise

STAY HYDRATED

- Drink water when you are thirsty. Light-colored urine indicates proper hydration, while dark-colored indicates dehydration.
- Water is the best thing you can drink—before, during, and after exercise or other outdoor activity.
- Consuming sports drinks with electrolytes can also be helpful, especially during and after intense exercise that causes a lot of sweating.
- Fruits and vegetables also provide electrolytes.
- Staying hydrated is just as important during winter activities. Bring water and a vacuum-insulated bottle for warm beverages.
- Bring enough for everyone, including kids and pets. Take into account the number of people as well as the types of activities. It is always better to have extra water available.

Extras

- ❏ Athletic tape
- ❏ Goalkeeper gloves
- ❏ Hair ties or headbands
- ❏ Indoor soccer shoes
- ❏ Popsicle sticks (to clean cleats)
- ❏ Practice clothes
- ❏ Slides
- ❏ Soccer studs
- ❏ Training balls
- ❏ Trash bag
- ❏ Turf shoes

SPORT CLIMBING, TRAD CLIMBING

Essentials

- ❏ Approach shoes
- ❏ Backpack
- ❏ Bandanna or buff
- ❏ Batteries and extra batteries for devices
- ❏ Belay/rappel device
- ❏ Belay/rappel gloves
- ❏ Binoculars
- ❏ Carabiners, locking and nonlocking
- ❏ Cell phone in protective bag
- ❏ Chalk and chalk bag
- ❏ Energy snacks, food, beverages
- ❏ Finger tape
- ❏ First-aid kit
- ❏ Harness
- ❏ Hat
- ❏ Headlamp or flashlight
- ❏ Helmet
- ❏ Hold brush
- ❏ Insect repellent
- ❏ Insulation: jacket, vest, other layers
- ❏ Knife or multi-tool

ORIENT TO THE SOUTHERN CROSS

- Imagine a line joining the two stars at the "head" and the "foot" of the Southern Cross.
- Extend the line out another four lengths from the foot of the cross to the south celestial pole.
- Then look straight down from the south celestial pole to the horizon. You've found south.

❏ Lip balm

❏ Multifunction watch or GPS

❏ Permits

❏ Quickdraws

❏ Rainwear

❏ Rock climbing shoes

❏ Rope

❏ Rope bag

❏ Route description or guidebook

❏ Runners, singles and doubles

❏ Shorts, pants, top

❏ Signaling mirror

❏ Slings and runners

❏ Stick clip

❏ Sunglasses and retainer strap

❏ Sunscreen

❏ Trip itinerary left with friend and also under car seat

❏ Water bottle(s)

THINGS TO BE HAPPY ABOUT OUTDOORS

- the summit
- goats climbing
- flowers blooming overnight
- lightning passing cloud to cloud
- the night sky

Sport Climbing Extras

- ❑ Camera
- ❑ Duffel
- ❑ Emergency reflective blanket
- ❑ Hand sanitizer
- ❑ Map and compass
- ❑ Notepad and pen or pencil
- ❑ Sanitation trowel
- ❑ Socks
- ❑ Toilet paper
- ❑ Trash bag
- ❑ Two-way radios
- ❑ Water treatment method
- ❑ Wicking T-shirt

Trad Climbing Extras

- ❐ Additional locking carabiners
- ❐ Cams
- ❐ Gear sling
- ❐ Hexes
- ❐ Map with protective case
- ❐ Matches, lighter, firestarter in waterproof container
- ❐ Nut extraction tool
- ❐ Nuts
- ❐ Repair kit
- ❐ Socks
- ❐ Trad protection for mixed routes

TENNIS

Essentials

- ❒ First-aid kit
- ❒ Hair ties or headband
- ❒ Hat or visor
- ❒ Racket bag
- ❒ Socks
- ❒ Sunglasses
- ❒ Sunscreen
- ❒ Tennis balls
- ❒ Tennis clothing
- ❒ Tennis racket
- ❒ Tennis shoes
- ❒ Towel
- ❒ Water bottle

Extras

- ❒ Athletic tape
- ❒ Ball hopper
- ❒ Grips
- ❒ Sweatbands

THINGS TO BE HAPPY ABOUT OUTDOORS

- hearing a barred owl
- a rodent chase
- a brightly colored flower in a crack in concrete
- birds building a nest
- a copse, or thicket, of small trees

ESTIMATE REMAINING DAYLIGHT

— Locate the sun and align the top of your outstretched hand (index finger on top, little finger closest to ground, palm facing you, and fingers parallel to horizon) with the sun's bottom edge.
— Position your index finger so that it is just below the sun.
— Count how many fingers it takes to the top of the horizon line.
— Each finger represents roughly 15 minutes of daylight remaining.
— One hand represents approximately 1 hour.
— You can line up your other hand directly below and continue counting.

TRACK AND FIELD

Essentials

- ❏ After-running shoes
- ❏ Cap or hat
- ❏ First-aid kit
- ❏ Hair ties or headband
- ❏ Lip balm
- ❏ Rainwear
- ❏ Running shoes or spikes
- ❏ Shorts
- ❏ Snacks
- ❏ Socks and extra socks
- ❏ Sunglasses
- ❏ Sunscreen
- ❏ Top and pants
- ❏ Towel
- ❏ Water bottle

Extras

- ❏ Gloves
- ❏ Jacket
- ❏ Skin lubricant
- ❏ Tights

THINGS TO BE HAPPY ABOUT OUTDOORS

- fresh air after a rain shower
- cherry blossoms
- a robin's welcome call
- the fragrance of cut grass
- a blue jay feather

MANAGE CHAFING

— Apply lubricant to high-friction areas on your body.
— Don't wear cotton. Go seamless and tagless. Make sure underwear and clothes fit properly.
— If wearing a pack, secure it so it does not bounce and shift, causing chafing.
— Stay hydrated because sweat and its salt irritates skin and can lead to chafing.
— If you are chafed, reduce the rubbing. Dry the problem area and apply a skin-treatment lubricant and/or change clothes.
— Take a shower as soon as you can, in lukewarm water, and pat dry.
— Treat chafing like a minor burn or diaper rash. Give the injured area time to heal.

TRIATHLON

Essentials

- ❏ After-race clothes and shoes
- ❏ Antifog solution for goggles
- ❏ Bicycle
- ❏ Bike helmet
- ❏ Bike tire pressure gauge
- ❏ Bike under-seat bag
- ❏ Body Glide or skin lubricant
- ❏ Cap or visor
- ❏ Cell phone
- ❏ Chamois cream
- ❏ CO2 inflator with cartridge or mini-pump
- ❏ Cycling footwear
- ❏ Cycling gloves
- ❏ Cycling shorts
- ❏ Cycling socks
- ❏ Cyclist's multi-tool
- ❏ Duffle
- ❏ Emergency contact card and medical info
- ❏ Energy drinks, snacks, food
- ❏ First-aid kit
- ❏ Floor pump
- ❏ Goggles and spare goggles
- ❏ Hat or visor
- ❏ Jersey, T-shirt, or other top
- ❏ Lip balm
- ❏ Medications
- ❏ Mirror for handlebar or helmet

THINGS TO BE HAPPY ABOUT OUTDOORS

- clover waking and rising
- tree branches talking and groaning
- daffodil sprouts
- morning clamor of birds
- the not-round sun

FIX A FLAT BIKE TIRE

(simplified version)

— Remove the wheel.
— Remove the tube: Deflate it completely and remove by pressing on the edge (bead) of the tire or by using a tire lever.
— Find the cause of the flat.
— Patch or replace the tube. You may prefer to replace the tube with a new one and fix the damaged one later.
— Reinstall the wheel.

❏ Patch kit and/or spare tube(s)

❏ Photo ID

❏ Pre-race footwear

❏ Race belt

❏ Race packet (number and documents)

❏ Recovery foods and drinks

❏ Running shoes

❏ Running socks

❏ Safety pins

❏ Speed laces

❏ Sunglasses (if different from cycling glasses)

❏ Sunscreen

❏ Tire changing supplies and levers

❏ Towel(s)

❏ Transition bags

❏ Tri suit or swimsuit

❏ Watch or heart rate monitor

❏ Water bottles or hydration pack

❏ Wetsuit

❏ Wipes and hand sanitizer

Extras

❏ Camera

❏ Earplugs

❏ Extra clothes

❏ Handlebar end caps

❏ Outerwear or rainwear

❏ Trash bag

VOLLEYBALL

Essentials

- ❑ Appropriate clothing: shorts, top/jersey, tights, sports bra
- ❑ Backpack or duffle bag

TAKE GOOD PHONE PICTURES

- Take advantage of natural light. Though you have flash on the phone, you should have it off in most cases.
- Know your camera. The default camera app for your phone has features that you should learn about using. You can adjust the exposure and lock a focal point and the exposure on most phones.
- Turn on the gridlines, which will make it easier to compose your photos and get the horizon line level. Use the rule of thirds to break up the image vertically and horizontally with the gridlines to get a more balanced picture.
- The timer is handy if you want to be included in a photo. The timer also helps in low light because even a slight movement of the phone can blur the image in that situation.
- When you take a photo in HDR (high dynamic range) mode, the camera takes several pictures at different exposures and then combines them to make a single image. Using HDR is especially effective when you are taking pictures of beautiful landscapes that have a range of color and brightness. HDR is not good, though, when you are photographing a subject in motion.
- Also play around with time-lapse, slo-mo, video, and panoramic on the camera.

- ❏ Elbow pads

- ❏ Hair ties or headband

- ❏ Knee pads

- ❏ Snacks

- ❏ Socks

- ❏ Volleyball

- ❏ Volleyball shoes

- ❏ Water bottle

Extras

- ❏ Ankle braces or sleeves

- ❏ Arm/passing sleeves

- ❏ Athletic tape and finger tape

- ❏ Ball pump

- ❏ Practice balls

WATER POLO

Essentials

- ❐ Backpack, duffle, or ball bag
- ❐ Mouthguard
- ❐ Swimsuit
- ❐ Towel
- ❐ Water polo caps

PURIFY WATER

— **Boil:** Bring water to a rolling boil for 3 to 5 minutes. Let cool before drinking.
— **Water purifier:** Use water purification and disinfection tablets. Follow the directions on the label or in the package to the letter.
— **Filter:** Use a portable water filter. Carefully follow the manufacturer's instructions for it.
— **Disinfect:** Make small quantities of water safer to drink by using chlorine bleach, iodine, or chlorine dioxide tablets. Follow the instructions to the letter.
— **Ultraviolet light:** Portable units that deliver a measured dose of UV light help disinfect small amounts of clear water. If the water is cloudy, it must be filtered before disinfecting with UV light.
— **Solar:** Fill a clean, clear plastic bottle with clear water. If the water is not clear, it must be filtered first. Lay the bottle on its side for 6 sunny hours or 2 cloudy days. Putting the bottle on a dark surface will help the sun's rays disinfect more effectively.

Extras

❏ Goggles or other eyewear

❏ Pump for ball

THINGS TO BE HAPPY ABOUT OUTDOORS

- a shooting star
- gulls riding the breezes
- a glorious flowering plant
- light falling through a tree
- a recognizable shape in the clouds

WATER SKIING

Essentials

- ❑ Boat
- ❑ Orange safety flag
- ❑ Personal flotation device (PDF) or life jacket
- ❑ Swimsuit
- ❑ Water ski bag
- ❑ Water ski gloves
- ❑ Water ski helmet
- ❑ Water skis
- ❑ Wetsuit

Extras

- ❑ Binding slime
- ❑ Bindings
- ❑ Dry suit

THINGS TO BE HAPPY ABOUT OUTDOORS

- baby ducks following mom
- water lapping the dock
- a spray or splash zone
- tidal pools with crabs
- seabirds wheeling and screeching

BOAT SAFELY IN A STORM

— Take waves at an angle.
— Secure loose items in the boat.
— Close all hatches and portals.
— Unplug electrical equipment.

❐ Spray leg guard

❐ Tow rope and handle

❐ Training skis

❐ Wing angle gauges

RECREATION

(defined as activities that are not rule-based and may be done as an individual or with others)

The first two lists—backpacking and bikepacking—are quite extensive. If, for example, you are combining an activity like fishing with backpacking or bike touring with hiking, please combine the two lists to make sure you have everything you need.

1. Backpacking

2. Bikepacking, Bicycle Touring

3. Canoeing

4. Cycling, Biking

5. Day Hiking

6. Disc Golf

7. Diving

8. Fishing

9. Frisbee

10. Geocaching

11. Hiking

12. Ice Skating

13. Inline Skating, Rollerblading, Roller Skating

14. Kayaking

15. Mountain Biking

16. Orienteering

17. Outdoor Exploration

18. Running, Jogging

19. Sailing

20. Skateboarding

21. Sledding, Tobogganing

22. Snowshoeing

23. Stand-Up Paddleboarding (SUP)

24. Surfing

25. Swimming

26. Ultimate Frisbee

27. Urban Hiking

28. Walking, Nordic Walking

29. Windsurfing

BACKPACKING

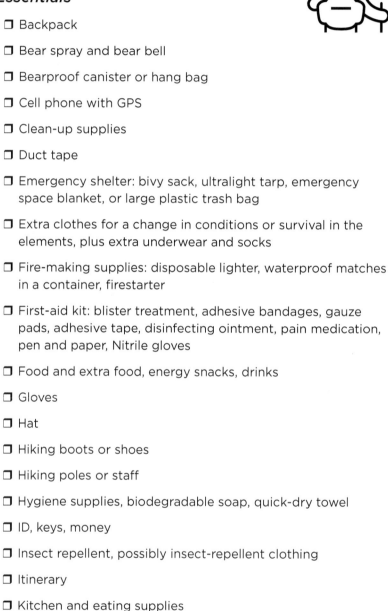

Essentials

- ❏ Backpack
- ❏ Bear spray and bear bell
- ❏ Bearproof canister or hang bag
- ❏ Cell phone with GPS
- ❏ Clean-up supplies
- ❏ Duct tape
- ❏ Emergency shelter: bivy sack, ultralight tarp, emergency space blanket, or large plastic trash bag
- ❏ Extra clothes for a change in conditions or survival in the elements, plus extra underwear and socks
- ❏ Fire-making supplies: disposable lighter, waterproof matches in a container, firestarter
- ❏ First-aid kit: blister treatment, adhesive bandages, gauze pads, adhesive tape, disinfecting ointment, pain medication, pen and paper, Nitrile gloves
- ❏ Food and extra food, energy snacks, drinks
- ❏ Gloves
- ❏ Hat
- ❏ Hiking boots or shoes
- ❏ Hiking poles or staff
- ❏ Hygiene supplies, biodegradable soap, quick-dry towel
- ❏ ID, keys, money
- ❏ Insect repellent, possibly insect-repellent clothing
- ❏ Itinerary
- ❏ Kitchen and eating supplies

- Knife: pocketknife or multi-tool
- Lighting: headlamp with batteries and extra batteries, or rechargeable flashlights or lanterns
- Navigation: some combination of map, compass, GPS device, altimeter watch, personal locator beacon (PLB) and/or satellite messenger
- Permits
- Prescription medication
- Rainwear
- Repair kit
- Sleeping bag and pad
- Stove and fuel

PITCH A TENT

— Find a good spot for your tent. Look for flat, level ground that is free of sticks or stumps.
— Lay out the footprint or a ground tarp.
— Lay out the body of the tent. Be sure the doors are facing the right direction, taking into account wind direction.
— Assemble the poles.
— Match the poles to the grommets on the tent body and footprint.
— Attach the tent body to the poles.
— Lay out the rain fly on top of the tent.
— Stake out the tent, corner by corner.
— Tighten up the rain fly.

THINGS TO BE HAPPY ABOUT OUTDOORS

- sunshine and shadow, damp coolness and shimmering heat
- a rock heap on a hilltop
- animal prints and tracks
- fish in the water
- wild fruit trees

❏ Sun protection: sunglasses, sunscreen, sun-protection clothing

❏ Tent, ground cloth, stakes, extra stakes

❏ Towel

❏ Water and extra water

❏ Water bottles

❏ Water treatment supplies

❏ Waterproof stuff sack

❏ Weather-appropriate clothing

Extras

❏ Bandanna or buff

❏ Binoculars

❏ Camera or action cam

❏ Camp shoes

❏ Daypack

❏ Field guide and star chart

❏ Gaiters

❏ Guidebook

- ☐ Handkerchief
- ☐ Journal with pen or pencil
- ☐ Pillow
- ☐ Reading material, cards, or games
- ☐ Tights
- ☐ Two-way radios
- ☐ Urinary products
- ☐ Windscreen for stove
- ☐ Zip-off hiking pants

BIKEPACKING, BICYCLE TOURING

Essentials

- ❏ Adjustable wrench (6-inch)
- ❏ Arm and leg warmers
- ❏ Assorted nuts and bolts
- ❏ Backpack
- ❏ Bike
- ❏ Bike lubricant
- ❏ Bike repair kit
- ❏ Brake and derailleur cables
- ❏ Buff, bandanna, cap, balaclava, or skullcap
- ❏ Camera
- ❏ Cargo rack plus trunk bag
- ❏ Cell phone with biking app
- ❏ Chain tool
- ❏ Chamois cream
- ❏ Clothing and extra clothing
- ❏ CO_2 inflator (with cartridges)
- ❏ Cooking and water filtration items
- ❏ Cycling computer or GPS
- ❏ Cycling multi-tool with Allen wrenches
- ❏ Cycling socks
- ❏ Duct tape
- ❏ Eye protection: sunglasses or clear lenses
- ❏ Fenders

- ☐ Fire-making supplies: disposable lighter, waterproof matches in a container, firestarter
- ☐ First-aid kit
- ☐ Food, snacks, beverages—and extras of all
- ☐ General purpose multi-tool
- ☐ Gloves, weatherproof and full-fingered
- ☐ Guidebook or route description
- ☐ Handlebar bag
- ☐ Hat
- ☐ Helmet and headlight
- ☐ Hydration pack
- ☐ Hygiene and toiletry items
- ☐ ID and money
- ☐ Insect repellent, possibly insect-repellent clothing
- ☐ Insulation layer(s)
- ☐ Lighting: headlamp with batteries and extra batteries, or rechargeable flashlights or lanterns
- ☐ Lip balm
- ☐ Lock
- ☐ Map and compass
- ☐ Medical info and emergency contact card

FIND THE EQUATOR IN A FOREST

- — Trees grow toward the sun, so branches will be thicker on the side facing the equator.
- — The rings on a stump will also grow more dense in the direction of the equator.

- ❑ Mirror for handlebar or helmet
- ❑ Off-day clothing
- ❑ Padded shorts or tights
- ❑ Panniers
- ❑ Prescription medication
- ❑ Pressure gauge
- ❑ Pump
- ❑ Rainwear
- ❑ Replacement chain links
- ❑ Saddle (underseat) bag
- ❑ Shelter and sleeping system
- ❑ Shoes suited to bike's pedals
- ❑ Small quick-dry towel
- ❑ Spare bike components
- ❑ Spare cleats
- ❑ Spare spokes and spoke wrench
- ❑ Spare tire
- ❑ Spare tube(s) and/or patch kit
- ❑ Stove and fuel

- ❏ Straps or bungee cords
- ❏ Sunscreen
- ❏ Taillight (with blinking option)
- ❏ Tent, ground cloth, stakes, extra stakes
- ❏ Tire levers
- ❏ Trailer
- ❏ Visibility vest
- ❏ Water bottle or hydration pack
- ❏ Wicking jersey or top
- ❏ Windbreaker (stowaway)

Extras

- ❏ Bandanna or buff
- ❏ Camera or action cam
- ❏ Camp shoes
- ❏ Emergency shelter: bivy sack, ultralight tarp, emergency space blanket, or large plastic trash bag
- ❏ Gaiters
- ❏ Handkerchief
- ❏ Journal with pen or pencil
- ❏ Pillow
- ❏ Reading material, cards, or games
- ❏ Tights
- ❏ Trailer
- ❏ Two-way radios
- ❏ Urinary products

CANOEING

Essentials

- ❏ Bailer or bilge pump
- ❏ Bailing wire
- ❏ Canoe
- ❏ Canoe paddles and extra one
- ❏ Canoe seat(s)
- ❏ Cell phone, ID, money in waterproof case
- ❏ Dry bags/box(es)
- ❏ Emergency floating throw line with throw bag
- ❏ Energy food and beverages
- ❏ Firestarter, matches, lighter in waterproof case
- ❏ First-aid kit
- ❏ Float bags
- ❏ Food and extra food
- ❏ GPS or multifunction watch
- ❏ Hat (sun-shielding)
- ❏ Hat or cap retainer
- ❏ Headlamp or flashlight and extra batteries
- ❏ Insect repellent
- ❏ Insulating clothing
- ❏ Knife or multi-tool
- ❏ Lip balm
- ❏ Maps, charts, compass in waterproof case
- ❏ Nylon cord or bungee cords
- ❏ Paddling apparel

- ❏ Paddling gloves
- ❏ Permits and licenses
- ❏ Personal flotation device (PDF) and extra one
- ❏ Putty
- ❏ Rainwear or spray jacket
- ❏ Repair kit, duct tape, replacement nuts and bolts
- ❏ Sealant
- ❏ Signaling devices: flares, mirror, strobe light, whistle
- ❏ Sponges
- ❏ Spray covers

WALK SAFELY IN A MARSH

- Wear shoes or boots that are laced up tightly and completely closed. Long pants and gloves are also recommended.
- Tidal creeks and salt marshes have a type of mud where you risk sinking in up to your waist and getting stuck.
- If this happens, the best way to escape is to lie on the mud surface and crawl to safety.
- Oyster shells are sharp and can cause severe cuts. Be very careful when walking on oyster reefs, and when walking in mud where the shells may be buried.
- Other types of brush with sharp, pointed tips grow in marshes. Be careful around these.
- Venomous snakes and alligators can also be found in salt marshes.
- It is important to know the local tides. Knowing what time high and low tide occur can prevent you from either being stranded or battling the tide to return to your starting point.

- ❏ Sunglasses
- ❏ Sunscreen
- ❏ Trip itinerary left with friend and also under car seat
- ❏ Water bottles
- ❏ Water shoes
- ❏ Water treatment method
- ❏ Weather radio
- ❏ Yoke with pads

Extras

- ❏ Bandanna or buff
- ❏ Binoculars
- ❏ Camera
- ❏ Convertible pants
- ❏ Cooler and ice
- ❏ Dry suit
- ❏ Duffels
- ❏ Fishing gear

THINGS TO BE HAPPY ABOUT OUTDOORS

- a cool mist rolling in over the waters
- a brief flap of wings as a bird rises from a nearby tree
- how the sun washes the earth
- a bullfrog in the cattails
- watching the mist lift

- ❏ Helmet
- ❏ Knee pads
- ❏ Moisture-wicking clothing
- ❏ Notebook and pen or pencil
- ❏ Rash guard
- ❏ Sandals or camp shoes
- ❏ Skullcap
- ❏ Swimsuit
- ❏ Synthetic handwear
- ❏ Toilet paper and waste collection bag
- ❏ Two-way radios
- ❏ Wetsuit

CYCLING, BIKING

Essentials

- ❏ Bike
- ❏ Cell phone
- ❏ Cycling apparel
- ❏ Cycling multi-tool with Allen wrenches
- ❏ Energy snacks
- ❏ Eye protection or sunglasses
- ❏ First-aid kit
- ❏ Helmet
- ❏ ID, keys, money, emergency contact info
- ❏ Lights and flashers
- ❏ Pump
- ❏ Saddle (underseat) bag
- ❏ Spare tube(s) and/or patch kit
- ❏ Sunscreen

BIKE REPAIR KIT

- — Bike tire pump
- — Duct tape
- — Lubrication supplies
- — Multi-tool
- — Patch kit and/or spare tube
- — Tire levers, Phillips and flat screwdrivers, Allen wrenches, open-end or adjustable wrench, spoke wrench, chain tool
- — Zip ties

- ❐ Tire levers
- ❐ Water bottle or hydration pack

Extras

- ❐ Bike lock
- ❐ Gloves
- ❐ Map
- ❐ Padded shorts
- ❐ Watch with biking app or bicycling computer
- ❐ Wicking top

THINGS TO BE HAPPY ABOUT OUTDOORS

- paw prints in the soil
- the geology of the area
- leaves just beginning to expand
- the moon's illumination
- gauzy streaks of cloud

DAY HIKING

Essentials

❏ Cell phone or watch with GPS

❏ Daypack, hip pack, or backpack

❏ First-aid kit

❏ Flashlight or headlamp with new batteries

❏ Gloves

TIPS FOR DAY HIKE

— Acquaint yourself with the area and specific trail(s) you plan to hike so you can set a reasonable timetable for your hike. Many guidebooks include estimated times of trips.

— Always carry plenty of water. Three quarts per person per day is a good rule of thumb. Warmer conditions and/or rugged terrain may necessitate carrying more.

— Carry more food than you think you will need. It is better to bring extra snacks home with you than to go hungry.

— Carrying your clothing and food in different-colored stuff sacks keeps your pack organized and helps you find your gear easily when you need it.

— Check weather conditions before you leave.

— Drink often to stay well hydrated. Purify water from natural sources.

- ❏ Hat
- ❏ Hiking footwear
- ❏ Hiking poles or staff
- ❏ ID, keys, money
- ❏ Insect repellent or insect-repellent clothing
- ❏ Jacket or windbreaker
- ❏ Knife or multi-tool
- ❏ Lunch and snacks

— Fill your canteens before you leave home. It is better to be prepared than to rely on backcountry water sources.

— Hike only as fast as the slowest member of your group.

— Leave your itinerary with someone you trust, and check in with them upon your return.

— Make sure your vehicle is in good running order and your gas tank is full.

— Note the time when you start your hike to gauge your pace and distance per hour.

— Practice minimum-impact hiking. Carry out whatever you pack in so others can enjoy the surroundings. Try to pick up what previous visitors may have left behind.

— Start off slowly to avoid excess fatigue partway through your hike.

— When you choose a hike, consider the ability levels of all members of your party.

❒ Map and compass

❒ Rainwear

❒ Sunglasses

❒ Sunscreen

❒ Trip itinerary left with family or friend and also under car seat

❒ Up-to-date weather forecast

❒ Water bottle(s)

❒ Weather-appropriate clothing

❒ Whistle or bear bell(s)

Extras

❒ Bandanna or buff

❒ Camera

❒ Clothes for warmer and cooler conditions

❒ Extra clothes

❒ Extra socks

❒ Emergency shelter

❏ Fire-making supplies

❏ Handkerchief

❏ Notebook and pen or pencil

❏ Tissues or toilet tissue

❏ Water treatment method

DISC GOLF

Essentials

- ❐ Cell phone (with disc golf app and GPS)
- ❐ Discs in carrying bag
- ❐ Extra socks
- ❐ Finger tape
- ❐ First-aid kit with Ace bandage
- ❐ Food, snacks, drinks
- ❐ Hiking shoes or boots (possibly waterproof)
- ❐ Insect repellent, possibly insect-repellent clothing
- ❐ Poison ivy wash and tick remover
- ❐ Rainwear
- ❐ Sunglasses
- ❐ Sunscreen
- ❐ Sweatshirt and windbreaker
- ❐ Towel
- ❐ Water bottle

THINGS TO BE HAPPY ABOUT OUTDOORS

- green lawns shaded by willows
- stars paling in the morning sky
- a robin hopping
- lavender in the breeze
- squirrels planting new trees

Extras

- ☐ After-golf shoes
- ☐ Camera
- ☐ Extra clothes, especially for wet weather
- ☐ Hydration pack
- ☐ Knee straps
- ☐ Stool or camp chair
- ☐ Toilet paper
- ☐ Umbrella

OUTDOOR ETIQUETTE

- — When on a trail or path, know your right-of-way. In many situations, those going uphill have the right-of-way.
- — Yield to horses and other pack animals.
- — Cyclists yield to hikers, walkers, horses, and other pack animals.
- — When you bring a pet along, be sure to keep it on a leash and under control.
- — Be friendly to others that you encounter.
- — When you approach someone from behind, make yourself known in a calm, friendly voice.
- — If you are on a trail or path, stay on it unless you are yielding or taking a break. If it is muddy or wet, try to walk through it instead of widening the trail.
- — Do what you can to protect the ecosystem. Do not disturb wildlife and keep your distance from wildlife you encounter.
- — Leave rocks, vegetation, and artifacts alone and in place so others can enjoy them.
- — Follow the Leave No Trace principles.

DIVING

Essentials

- ❏ Boat bag
- ❏ Buoyancy compensator
- ❏ Buoyancy control device (with alternate air source and integrated weight pockets)
- ❏ Cell phone in waterproof container
- ❏ Certification log and book
- ❏ Clothes
- ❏ Defog
- ❏ Diarrhea medication
- ❏ Dive beacon
- ❏ Dive computer
- ❏ Dive flag
- ❏ Dive light (with lanyard)
- ❏ Dive skin
- ❏ Dive weight
- ❏ Dry box
- ❏ Dry suit

THINGS TO BE HAPPY ABOUT OUTDOORS

- hearing a duck whistle
- surf on a sandy shore
- dead invertebrates
- sunken treasure
- the underside of a wave

- ❑ Fins and booties
- ❑ First-aid kit
- ❑ Flashlight and extra batteries
- ❑ Food and extra food
- ❑ Gear bag
- ❑ Hat or visor
- ❑ ID in waterproof container
- ❑ Insect repellent
- ❑ Knife
- ❑ Mask
- ❑ Mesh weight belt
- ❑ Plastic bags, various sizes
- ❑ Prescription medication
- ❑ Pressure gauge, depth gauge, compass, dive computer (or dive console)
- ❑ Recreational dive planner (wheel, tables, or ERDP)
- ❑ Regulator with alternate air source
- ❑ Scuba or reef gloves
- ❑ Scuba tank
- ❑ Sea band acupressure pads
- ❑ Seasickness/nausea medication
- ❑ Snacks
- ❑ Snorkel
- ❑ Sunglasses
- ❑ Sunscreen
- ❑ Surface marker buoy
- ❑ Swimmer's ear solution
- ❑ Swimsuit(s)

SWIM TO SHORE

- Choose a large landmark so that you can easily keep swimming toward it.
- In the ocean, you'll feel the swell around you. The waves will give you a natural lift. Use the swell and follow its direction. Increase your stroke and kick effort to run with the swell.
- Sighting backward is just as important as sighting forward. It lets you know exactly where the waves are. You can either avoid them or connect with them— bodysurf the wave or whitewash.
- If at some point you don't think you can make it to shore, start calling and waving to draw attention to yourself.
- When you are close to shore, avoid standing up too soon. You might get pulled back. Continue swimming to shore until the water is no deeper than your waist.

❐ Toiletries

❐ Towel

❐ Trip itinerary left with someone and also under vehicle seat

❐ Underwater camera

❐ Underwater slate and pencil

❐ Water shoes

❐ Wetsuit

❐ Windbreaker

Extras

- ❐ Batteries and extra batteries for flashlight
- ❐ Dive compass
- ❐ Dive lights
- ❐ Diving knife
- ❐ Lamps for flashlight
- ❐ Mask and fin straps
- ❐ O-rings
- ❐ Regulator mouthpiece
- ❐ Snorkel keeper
- ❐ Tank bangers

FISHING

Essentials

- ❏ Boots or waders
- ❏ Cell phone in protective case
- ❏ Clothes for warmer and cooler conditions
- ❏ Compass
- ❏ Cooler
- ❏ Dry cases and bags
- ❏ Duct tape
- ❏ First-aid kit
- ❏ Fishing license
- ❏ Fishing net
- ❏ Fishing vest
- ❏ Gloves, fingerless
- ❏ GPS
- ❏ Hat
- ❏ Insect repellent, netting, insect-repellent clothing
- ❏ Line
- ❏ Lip balm
- ❏ Live bait
- ❏ Lures, hooks, sinkers, jigs, spoons, flies
- ❏ Map of body of water and area
- ❏ Multi-tool, knife, pliers
- ❏ Quick-dry towel
- ❏ Rainwear
- ❏ Rod and reel
- ❏ Snacks and energy bars
- ❏ Spare batteries for devices
- ❏ Sunglasses

THINGS TO BE HAPPY ABOUT OUTDOORS

- foliage along waterways
- a quiet pool in a gurgling stream
- the pastiche of a colorful village
- clouds merging and fraying
- a great rock to fish from

- ❏ Sunscreen
- ❏ Tackle case
- ❏ Water bottle

Extras

- ❏ Backing for line
- ❏ Bandanna or balaclava
- ❏ Camera
- ❏ Emergency shelter
- ❏ Extra clothes
- ❏ Extra food
- ❏ Fire-making supplies
- ❏ Hand sanitizer
- ❏ Rope tape measurer
- ❏ Toilet paper or wipes
- ❏ Water treatment method

TOAST FOOD ON A STICK

- — A plain stick will do. You can cook bread, bacon, pretty much anything on a stick.
- — Always use wood that is safe to cook with. Avoid scrap wood that has been painted or varnished. Greenwood sticks generally work best, as they are less likely to catch fire and burn through.
- — Dry ash, beech, hazel, oak, and willow will burn for a long time. Apple, cherry, plum, and other fruit trees are also good.
- — Spruce and pine are better as firestarters rather than cookers. They impart resin and also burn very hot and fast. Pretty much stay away from all conifers, including cedar, cypress, and hemlock.
- — Choose a stick that is long enough to enable you to sit safely away from the fire.
- — Whittle off the bark at the end so you have a nice, clean, smooth area and a sharp tip.

FRISBEE

Essentials

- ❏ Appropriate clothes
- ❏ Clothes for weather and change of weather
- ❏ Food, snacks, beverages
- ❏ Frisbees
- ❏ ID, keys, money

EXERCISE WITH NATURAL OBJECTS

- Hug a narrow tree trunk and do squats, bottom out and knees bending. Hold a full squat or pulse shorter ones.
- Use a park bench (in good repair) to do step-ups or pushups.
- Find a log with a fairly flat side facing up. Do box jumps, rapidly stepping onto and off the log, alternating feet.
- Use a secured park bench to do angled pushups against the back. With a park bench that is not anchored, do the angled pushups by putting your hands on the seat.
- Use a bench or table to do upper arm dips with your back to the object, lowering yourself until your arms are bent about 90 degrees.
- Natural weights like loose rocks, branches, or small logs can be used to do upper and lower body exercises. Just make sure that if you are using two, they are of fairly equal weight.

- ☐ Insect repellent
- ☐ Rainwear
- ☐ Shoes with cleats or good traction
- ☐ Sunglasses
- ☐ Sunscreen
- ☐ Towel
- ☐ Water bottle(s)

Extras

- ☐ After-play shoes
- ☐ Cleats
- ☐ Cones
- ☐ Disc clip
- ☐ Gloves
- ☐ Hygiene supplies
- ☐ Leggings or tights
- ☐ Pads and braces
- ☐ Trash bag

THINGS TO BE HAPPY ABOUT OUTDOORS

- encountering a stone wall in deep woods
- the wandering moon
- sunshine on your face
- a small plant, growing
- the squush of mud

GEOCACHING

Essentials

- ❏ Backpack
- ❏ Camera
- ❏ Cell phone with GPS or a GPS device
- ❏ Clamp tool
- ❏ Compass
- ❏ Duct tape
- ❏ Emergency space blanket
- ❏ Extra logbooks, pencils, pens, containers
- ❏ First-aid kit with poison oak/ivy spray
- ❏ Flashlight and extra batteries
- ❏ Forceps
- ❏ Gloves
- ❏ Hand sanitizer
- ❏ Hiking boots or sturdy shoes
- ❏ Insect repellent, maybe insect-repellent clothing
- ❏ Logbook
- ❏ Magnet, telescoping
- ❏ Matches, waterproof

WALK A STRAIGHT LINE IN THE WOODS

It is often difficult to walk a straight line in the wilderness due to uneven terrain and obstacles. Follow these tips:

- Choose your direction.
- Find a landmark in/on that route.
- Walk toward the landmark.
- Arrive, then choose a new landmark.
- Another method is to line up three objects in a straight line, with you at the center, then walk to the next object and that becomes the new center. This helps you bypass optical illusions caused by curves on the land.

- ❑ Mirror, small
- ❑ Multi-tool
- ❑ Needlenose pliers
- ❑ Paper towels
- ❑ Pen and pencil
- ❑ Penlight
- ❑ Phone charger or extra phone batteries
- ❑ Pocketknife
- ❑ Rainwear or emergency poncho

- ❑ Road atlas or map
- ❑ Snacks and extra snacks or food
- ❑ Sunglasses
- ❑ Sunscreen
- ❑ Swag for trading
- ❑ Trash bag
- ❑ Tweezers (for micro/nano logs)
- ❑ Walking stick or trekking pole
- ❑ Water bottle(s)

Extras

- ❑ Coat hanger, metal
- ❑ Emergency poncho
- ❑ Emergency space blanket
- ❑ Extra clothes
- ❑ Eye protection: safety glasses
- ❑ Firestarter and matches

- ❑ Fishing hook on a string
- ❑ Head protection
- ❑ Paper towels
- ❑ Shoes for after geocaching
- ❑ Tick remover
- ❑ Toilet paper
- ❑ Whistle

HIKING

Essentials

- ❐ Backpack or daypack
- ❐ Bear bell and bear spray
- ❐ Cell phone with GPS
- ❐ Compass
- ❐ Emergency shelter
- ❐ Extra clothes and socks
- ❐ Fire-making supplies
- ❐ First-aid kit
- ❐ Flashlight or headlamp and extra batteries
- ❐ Food and snacks, and extra food
- ❐ Gloves
- ❐ Hat or cap
- ❐ Hiking boots or shoes
- ❐ Hiking poles or staff
- ❐ ID, keys, money
- ❐ Insect repellent, possibly insect-repellent clothing
- ❐ Itinerary left with family or friend and also under car seat
- ❐ Jacket or pullover
- ❐ Map or guidebook
- ❐ Notebook and pencil or pen
- ❐ Pocketknife or multi-tool
- ❐ Rainwear
- ❐ Sunglasses or hat with visor
- ❐ Sunscreen
- ❐ Up-to-date weather forecast

THINGS TO BE HAPPY ABOUT OUTDOORS

- your first step onto the trail
- the musty organic odor of marsh
- slender young tree trunks
- baby birds hopping
- large rocks with long shadows

NAVIGATE WITHOUT A COMPASS

— Use the sun and stars to find north.
— Use trail blazes and markers.
— Learn to read topographical (topo) maps and find your position using map details.
— Use big landmarks to track your location.
— Follow the edges of a body of water.
— Learn to walk a straight line in a forest.
— Employ the general awareness method, using all your senses.
— Remember the sun rises in the east and sets in the west.

❐ Water bottles(s) or hydration pack

❐ Water treatment supplies

❐ Whistle

Extras

❐ Bandanna or buff

❐ Binoculars

❐ Camera

❐ Duct tape

❐ Gaiters

❐ Handkerchief

❐ Hygiene supplies

❐ Prescription medication

❐ Toilet tissue

❐ Urinary products

❐ Ziplock bags

❐ Zip-off hiking pants

ICE SKATING

Essentials

- ❑ Buff or scarf
- ❑ Cell phone
- ❑ Gloves or mittens
- ❑ Hat
- ❑ Helmet
- ❑ Ice skate covers and guards
- ❑ Ice skates
- ❑ Laces
- ❑ Layered clothing
- ❑ Pants or leggings/tights
- ❑ Shoes
- ❑ Skate bag
- ❑ Snacks, food, hot drinks
- ❑ Socks
- ❑ Water bottle

THINGS TO BE HAPPY ABOUT OUTDOORS

- stars peeking from behind clouds
- quiet woodland nooks
- sunlight warming a plant
- pogonip
- a reflection of a bird in flight

Extras

- ❏ Camera
- ❏ Elbow pads
- ❏ Hip pads
- ❏ Ice skating soakers
- ❏ ID, keys, money
- ❏ Knee pads or braces
- ❏ Protective glasses
- ❏ Unitard
- ❏ Wrist guards

HELP SOMEONE OUT OF AN ICE HOLE

- — Anchor yourself.
- — Crawl out to the hole with a stick.
- — Let the victim take hold of the stick.
- — Pull while the victim kicks out.

INLINE SKATING, ROLLERBLADING, ROLLER SKATING

Essentials

- ❑ Elbow pads

- ❑ First-aid kit

- ❑ Gloves

- ❑ Helmet

- ❑ Mouthguard

- ❑ Padded shorts/bottom

- ❑ Pads: elbow, knee, wrist

BLISTER PREVENTION

- — Don't cut corners on footwear or socks. Make sure your shoes fit right. Wear socks that wick away moisture or do not increase sweating. Wool or polyester are recommended.
- — Always pack an extra pair of socks to ensure your feet stay dry and clean.
- — Make sure your socks do not slip up and down while you walk.
- — Your footwear should be broken in.
- — Toughen your skin by wearing the socks and shoes in other situations, not just for the sport or recreational activity.
- — Consider using a quality lubricant on your feet to reduce friction. Stay away from powder or use it sparingly.

THINGS TO BE HAPPY ABOUT OUTDOORS

- geese in V-formations
- a turtle crossing the road
- seagulls wheeling above
- warm breezes
- gardens in full bloom

❐ Skate bag

❐ Skates

❐ Socks

❐ Water bottle

❐ Wrist guards

Extras

❐ Eye protection or sunglasses

❐ Sunscreen

❐ Towel

KAYAKING

Essentials

- ❏ Cell phone, ID, money in waterproof case
- ❏ Clothing layers for changing conditions
- ❏ Cord
- ❏ Dry bags/box(es)
- ❏ Dry suit
- ❏ Energy food and beverages
- ❏ First-aid kit
- ❏ GPS and/or multifunction watch
- ❏ Hat with brim and hat retainer
- ❏ Headlamp or flashlight
- ❏ Insect repellent
- ❏ Kayak
- ❏ Kayak paddles and spare
- ❏ Knife or multi-tool
- ❏ Lip balm
- ❏ Maps and charts in waterproof case
- ❏ Paddle float and leash
- ❏ Paddling apparel
- ❏ Paddling gloves
- ❏ Paddling shoes
- ❏ Personal flotation device (PDF) and extra one
- ❏ Rainwear
- ❏ Spray skirt
- ❏ Sunglasses
- ❏ Sunscreen
- ❏ Tide information
- ❏ Toilet paper

THINGS TO BE HAPPY ABOUT OUTDOORS

- the cry of a loon
- trees dancing in the wind
- the patchwork of clouds
- a beaver's dam
- rainbows on river water

RIGHT A CAPSIZED KAYAK

- Reach under your kayak and grab on to both sides of the cockpit rim. Push it over and flip it upright.
- Once your kayak is upright, reach across to the opposite side of it and pull your body up and onto it— as if you were getting out of a swimming pool.

❐ Trip itinerary left with friend and also under car seat

❐ Water shoes

❐ Whistle

Extras

❐ Bailer or bilge pump

❐ Bailing wire

❐ Extra batteries for devices

❐ Firestarter, matches, lighter in waterproof case

❐ Float bags

❐ Food and extra food

❐ Large sponge

❐ Personal locator beacon

❐ Putty

❐ Repair kit and duct tape

❐ Sealant

❐ Signaling devices: flares, mirror, strobe light

❐ Spray covers

❐ Swimsuit

❐ Water treatment method

❐ Weather radio

❐ Wetsuit

MOUNTAIN BIKING

Essentials

❐ Bike, mountain

❐ Buff or skullcap

❐ Cell phone

❐ Chamois cream

❐ Clothing and layered protection for weather

❐ Compact pump

❐ Compass

❐ Cycling computer and/or GPS

❐ Cycling multi-tool

❐ Cycling socks

❐ Eye protection or sunglasses

❐ First-aid kit

❐ Food, energy snacks, drinks

❐ Footwear suited to bike's pedals

❐ Gloves, weatherproof

❐ Headlight and flashlight

❐ Helmet

❐ ID, medical information, keys, money

❐ Insect repellent

❐ Maps, guidebook, route description

❐ Padded shorts, pants, or tights

- ❏ Pads and guards: elbow, knee, shin, upper body, wrist
- ❏ Patch kit and/or spare tube(s)
- ❏ Personal care (toiletries) or clean-up kit
- ❏ Rainwear
- ❏ Saddle or handlebar bag
- ❏ Shoes for after biking
- ❏ Sunscreen
- ❏ Taillight
- ❏ Tire levers
- ❏ Towel, small quick-dry
- ❏ Trailhead permit if needed
- ❏ Water bottles or hydration pack
- ❏ Weatherproof gloves
- ❏ Whistle
- ❏ Windbreaker, stowaway

Extras

- ❏ Additional fix-it and safety items
- ❏ Additional items depending on your ride: e.g., gloves or lock
- ❏ Additional water and food
- ❏ Arm and leg warmers
- ❏ Bike lock
- ❏ Camera
- ❏ Clothes for after biking

❐ Emergency shelter

❐ Fire-making supplies

❐ Lip balm

❐ Toilet paper

❐ Water treatment supplies

❐ Wrist altimeter

THINGS TO BE HAPPY ABOUT OUTDOORS

- the scent of rain bouncing up off fertile ground
- seed puffs blowing through the air
- the humming of small insects
- animals aimlessly taking their time
- branches with new growth

SIGNAL PROPERLY ON A BIKE

- Signal right turns by turning your left arm up at a right (90-degree) angle. The hand points up and palm faces forward.
- Alternatively, you can signal right turns by extending your right arm straight right.
- Signal left turns by extending your left arm straight left. All fingers can be extended left or point left with your index finger.
- Signal stopping or slowing by extending your left arm at a right (90-degree) angle facing downward and your palm facing backward.
- Alternatively, you can signal stopping or slowing by extending your right arm at a right (90-degree) angle facing downward and your palm facing backwards.
- If you are riding in a group, point to and call out hazards to other cyclists.

ORIENTEERING

Essentials

- ❐ Backpack
- ❐ Camera
- ❐ Cell phone with GPS
- ❐ Compasses, two orienteering type
- ❐ Extra phone batteries or phone charger
- ❐ First-aid kit with poison oak/ivy spray
- ❐ Food and extra food and snacks
- ❐ Gloves
- ❐ Hiking boots or shoes or trail runners
- ❐ Instructions and control card
- ❐ Map in case
- ❐ Outdoor clothing and layers
- ❐ Pencil and pen, waterproof
- ❐ Pocketknife or multi-tool
- ❐ Rainwear or emergency poncho
- ❐ Sunglasses

ORIENT A MAP

— Place your compass on the map with the direction-of-travel arrow (usually a red triangle) pointing toward the top of the map.
— Rotate the bezel so that the N of the compass is lined up with the direction-of-travel arrow.
— Slide the baseplate until one of its straight edges aligns with either the left or right edge of the map. (The direction-of-travel arrow should still be pointing toward the top of the map.)
— While holding the map and compass steady, rotate your body until the end of the magnetic needle (usually red) is within the outline of the orienting arrow. The map is now oriented correctly.

- ☐ Sunscreen
- ☐ Tarp, waterproof blanket, or towel
- ☐ Walking stick or trekking poles
- ☐ Water bottle and extra water
- ☐ Whistle

Extras

- ☐ Duct tape
- ☐ Emergency poncho
- ☐ Emergency space blanket
- ☐ Extra clothes
- ☐ Eye protection
- ☐ Firestarter and matches
- ☐ Gaiters
- ☐ Hand sanitizer
- ☐ Head protection
- ☐ Headlamp or flashlight and extra batteries
- ☐ Logbook/notebook
- ☐ Paper towels
- ☐ Shoes for after orienteering
- ☐ Tick remover
- ☐ Toilet paper
- ☐ Trash bag

THINGS TO BE HAPPY ABOUT OUTDOORS

- geological factors sculpting the landscape
- green shoots of new plants
- gangly moose
- nuts and seeds ripening
- wild turkeys

OUTDOOR EXPLORATION

Essentials

- ❑ Appropriate clothing and footwear
- ❑ Cell phone
- ❑ Daypack or backpack
- ❑ Emergency bivy
- ❑ Firestarter
- ❑ First-aid kit
- ❑ Food and snacks
- ❑ Insect repellent
- ❑ Itinerary left with someone and also under vehicle seat
- ❑ Knife or multi-tool
- ❑ Lighting: headlamp, flashlight, lantern
- ❑ Map and compass or GPS
- ❑ Rainwear
- ❑ Sunglasses
- ❑ Sunscreen
- ❑ Water
- ❑ Water treatment system

Extras

- ❑ Bandanna or buff
- ❑ Binoculars
- ❑ Camera
- ❑ Field guide(s)
- ❑ Gloves or mittens
- ❑ Hand sanitizer

THINGS TO BE HAPPY ABOUT OUTDOORS

- gray squirrels chattering
- a wildflower meadow
- the orbital motions of Earth
- the shine of wet leaves
- a small island in a river or lake

BASIC OUTDOOR CLOTHING

- Bottoms/pants
- Camp shoes or flip-flops
- Down or synthetic jacket or vest
- Extra clothes, socks, shoes
- Gloves and/or mittens
- Hiking or trail running shoes or boots
- Hiking pants, convertible pants, and/or shorts
- Hoodie sweatshirt, sweater, or fleece jacket
- Pajamas
- Rain or wind jacket and rain pants
- Socks
- Sports bra or jock strap
- Sun hat, beanie, bandanna, balaclava, or buff
- T-shirt
- Top, long-sleeve and wicking
- Underwear
- Wind shirt
- Work gloves

❐ Hiking footwear

❐ Lip balm

❐ Magnifier

❐ Phone charger or extra phone batteries

❐ Trekking poles

RUNNING, JOGGING

Essentials

- ❐ Cell phone
- ❐ First-aid kit
- ❐ Flashlight or headlamp
- ❐ GPS or map and compass
- ❐ Hat or visor
- ❐ ID, keys, money
- ❐ Layers and a shell
- ❐ Multifunction or GPS watch
- ❐ Pocketknife or multi-tool
- ❐ Rainwear
- ❐ Reflective vest or other reflective items
- ❐ Running backpack, vest, waistbelt, or waist pack
- ❐ Running or trail running shoes
- ❐ Running pants or shorts
- ❐ Safety whistle
- ❐ Shirt or wicking top
- ❐ Small towel
- ❐ Snacks, energy bars, drinks
- ❐ Socks and extra socks
- ❐ Speed laces
- ❐ Sports bra or supporter
- ❐ Sunglasses
- ❐ Sunscreen
- ❐ Tissues
- ❐ Trash bag
- ❐ Water bottle or hydration pack
- ❐ Windbreaker

THINGS TO BE HAPPY ABOUT OUTDOORS

- a rose's scent
- the pink tinge of a sunrise
- clouds arranged and rearranged
- trees admiring their shadows
- a pond thawing

PERSONAL HYGIENE KIT

- Alarm clock or phone/ watch with alarm
- Bath towels
- Biodegradable soap, baby wipes, hand sanitizer
- Brush or comb
- Cell phone and charger
- Cosmetics, waterproof
- Deodorant
- Face towel
- Fast-dry pack towel
- Insect repellent
- Keys to house and car
- Lip balm
- Lotion
- Razor and shaving cream
- Shampoo
- Sunglasses and case
- Sunscreen
- Toilet paper in resealable bag
- Toiletry bag
- Toothbrush
- Toothpaste
- Wallet with ID, credit cards, cash
- Watch

Extras

- ☐ Bandanna, buff, or balaclava
- ☐ Ear muffs
- ☐ Extra batteries
- ☐ Gloves or mittens
- ☐ Hand and feet warmers
- ☐ Headlamp with fresh charge or extra batteries
- ☐ Heart rate monitor
- ☐ Insect repellent
- ☐ Lip balm
- ☐ Route description
- ☐ Running gaiters
- ☐ Running jacket
- ☐ Sun sleeves
- ☐ Technical socks
- ☐ Thermal underwear
- ☐ Topo map

SAILING

Essentials

- ❒ Anchoring gloves
- ❒ Arrival/departure checklists
- ❒ Binoculars
- ❒ Blanket(s)
- ❒ Boat shoes
- ❒ Bungee cords, assorted
- ❒ Can opener
- ❒ Chargers for devices
- ❒ Charts
- ❒ Clothing for weather and change of weather
- ❒ Cooler (drain plug closed)
- ❒ Drawing compass
- ❒ Dry suit
- ❒ Duct tape
- ❒ Eating utensils
- ❒ First-aid kit
- ❒ Flashlight
- ❒ Float plan
- ❒ Food and drink, and extra
- ❒ Hand sanitizer and wipes
- ❒ Hand-bearing compass
- ❒ Handheld spotlight, fully charged, and chargers
- ❒ Hat and hat retainer
- ❒ Heaving line

THINGS TO BE HAPPY ABOUT OUTDOORS
- night unmarred by lights
- wading through warm ripples
- dabbling ducks
- silence on every side
- the tumbling well of space

❏ ID, emergency contacts, keys, money

❏ Itinerary left with someone and also under vehicle seat

❏ Knives

❏ Knotstick

❏ Light list

❏ Line, dacron

❏ Line, nylon

❏ Log book

❏ Matches, waterproof

❏ Multi-tool

❏ Paper napkins

❏ Parallel rule

❏ Pencil, pen, eraser

❏ Personal flotation devices (Type III with whistles)

❏ Plastic cold cups

❏ Pot holders

❏ Radar reflector

❏ Rainwear

❏ Rigging knives

- ❏ Sailing gloves
- ❏ Slide rule
- ❏ Sneakers with nonslip soles
- ❏ Spare winch handle
- ❏ Strobes for lifejackets/PDFs
- ❏ Sunglasses
- ❏ Sunscreen
- ❏ Swim goggles
- ❏ Swimsuit(s)
- ❏ Tide and sunrise/sunset tables
- ❏ Towels
- ❏ Trash bags and ziplock bags
- ❏ Vise grips
- ❏ Water and extra water
- ❏ Water shoes
- ❏ Water treatment supplies
- ❏ Waterproof watch

SLEEP ON THE BEACH

- — Don't bring glass bottles.
- — A tarp lean-to provides shade.
- — Camp well above the line of debris marking high tide.
- — Use damp sand to scrub dishes.
- — Weight tent lines and bury in sand instead of using spikes.
- — Keep towels and a brush handy at the tent's opening.
- — Fully extinguish fires.

- ❏ Wetsuit and gloves
- ❏ Wire cutters

Extras

- ❏ Clothes for other purposes during trip
- ❏ Flashlight on a rope
- ❏ Games or reading material
- ❏ Glasses/sunglasses retainer strap
- ❏ Hygiene products
- ❏ Navigation/nautical chart dividers
- ❏ Power pack for devices
- ❏ Prescription medication
- ❏ Rash guards
- ❏ Snorkeling gear
- ❏ Spray top or smock
- ❏ Take-ashore bag or backpack
- ❏ Underwater camera
- ❏ Whiteboard and marker

SKATEBOARDING

Essentials

- ❏ Cell phone or smartwatch
- ❏ Crash pants
- ❏ Elbow pads
- ❏ Eye protection
- ❏ First-aid kit
- ❏ Helmet
- ❏ Knee pads
- ❏ Skateboard
- ❏ Skateboarding shoes or flat, grippy-sole sneakers
- ❏ Slide gloves
- ❏ Water bottle
- ❏ Wrist guards

LACE SHOES

— The reef knot is more secure than the granny knot, which is the simple shoelace knot we all learned as kids. To test that, tie your shoes. If the loop ends skew slightly so that at least one loop is down rather than directly sideways, you tied a not-so-dependable granny knot.

— To tie a reef knot, cross and snug the laces, then form your first loop the same way.

— Now, reverse the path of the lace as you form your second loop; if you always pass the lace on top of the first loop, then pass it under the second loop this time (or vice versa). This is the step that fixes the knot.

Extras

- ☐ Bearings
- ☐ Daypack
- ☐ Grip tape
- ☐ Risers or shock pads
- ☐ Skateboarding trucks
- ☐ Snacks and food
- ☐ Spare parts
- ☐ Towel
- ☐ Wheels

THINGS TO BE HAPPY ABOUT OUTDOORS

- cottage gardens
- a field of corn
- wind combing blades of grass
- a flock of birds rising up
- flowers' strong scent

SLEDDING, TOBOGGANING

Essentials

- ❏ Active winter clothing (in layers)
- ❏ Boots, waterproof and insulated
- ❏ Eye protection: goggles or sunglasses
- ❏ First-aid kit
- ❏ Gloves or mittens and extras
- ❏ Hat or balaclava
- ❏ Helmet
- ❏ Long underwear or tights
- ❏ Neck gaiter (buff)
- ❏ Sled or toboggan
- ❏ Snacks and food
- ❏ Socks, wool
- ❏ Vacuum bottle with hot liquids
- ❏ Water bottle

THINGS TO BE HAPPY ABOUT OUTDOORS

- snowdrops under a tree
- bright white clouds
- Earth's horizon
- hills to climb
- boughs creaking

PITCH A SNOW CAMP

- Pack down a flat spot with skis or something else flat, then pitch the tent on top.
- Tie tent lines to rocks and bury in the snow.
- Dig a pit at the tent opening for putting on and removing boots.
- Don't pitch the tent in avalanche-prone areas.
- Don't use a campstove inside a tent.
- Run melted snow through a coffee filter before drinking.

Extras

- ❏ Camera
- ❏ Cell phone or smartwatch
- ❏ Daypack or lumbar pack
- ❏ Extra clothes
- ❏ Extra socks
- ❏ Foot warmers
- ❏ Hand warmers
- ❏ Liner gloves
- ❏ Liner socks
- ❏ Lip balm
- ❏ Shoes for after activity

SNOWSHOEING

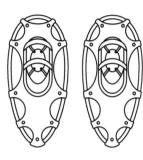

Essentials

- ❏ Active winter clothing (in layers)
- ❏ Boots, waterproof and insulated
- ❏ Daypack or lumbar pack
- ❏ First-aid kit
- ❏ Gloves or mittens and extras
- ❏ Hat or balaclava
- ❏ Neck gaiter (buff)

SIGNAL FOR HELP

— Call for help on your cell phone or use a personal locator beacon.
— Blow a whistle. Alternatively, beat and bang on things.
— Use a signal mirror (or any reflective surface), sweeping the mirror very slowly right to left and up and down.
— Set off a handheld flare or flare gun.
— Create a bright-colored flag with clothing or survey tape and tie it to a tall stick or pole, or anything tall.
— Make a signal fire in a visible place, but make sure it is under control.
— Use dark logs or rocks to spell out HELP, SOS, X, or V.
— Never rely on one method. Use numerous different methods to shorten response time.
— Use the single-handed gesture to alert others that you feel threatened and need help: Hold your hand up with your thumb tucked into your palm, then fold your fingers down, trapping the thumb in your fingers.

❏ Snacks and food

❏ Snowshoes

❏ Socks, wool, and extras

❏ Trekking poles

❏ Vacuum bottle with hot liquids

❏ Water bottle

Extras

❏ Cell phone or smartwatch

❏ Foot warmers

❏ Gaiters

❏ Hand warmers

❏ Liner gloves

❏ Liner socks

❏ Lip balm

❏ Long underwear or tights

❏ Sunglasses

❏ Sunscreen

STAND-UP PADDLEBOARDING (SUP)

Essentials

- ❏ Board shorts or swimsuit
- ❏ Cell phone in protective case or waterproof smartwatch
- ❏ Clothing for water temperature (not air temperature)
- ❏ Compass that floats
- ❏ Deck bag or dry bags
- ❏ Fin(s) for SUP
- ❏ First-aid kit
- ❏ Flashlight, waterproof
- ❏ GPS
- ❏ Guidebook, maps, charts in waterproof case
- ❏ Hat retainer
- ❏ Healthy snacks and beverages
- ❏ Knife or multi-tool
- ❏ Lip balm
- ❏ Paddling gloves
- ❏ Personal flotation device (PFD)
- ❏ Safety whistle
- ❏ Stand-up paddleboard
- ❏ Sun-protective shirt or rash guard

STAND UP ON A PADDLEBOARD

- — Carry the board into the water and start out on your knees or lying on your stomach.
- — From a kneeling position, move your feet to where your knees are.
- — Stand up by raising your chest and extending your legs.
- — Stand over the carry handle with your knees slightly bent and feet hip-width distance apart to balance and stay stable.

❐ Sun-shielding hat

❐ Sunglasses and retainer strap

❐ Sunscreen

❐ SUP carry strap

❐ SUP leash

❐ SUP paddle

❐ SUP transport cart

❐ Towel

❐ Towline

❐ Water bottle(s) or hydration reservoir/waistpack

❐ Water shoes or sandals

❐ Weather radio

Extras

❐ Boots

❐ Emergency blanket

❐ Gloves

❐ Headlamp

❐ Insect repellent

❐ Neoprene top and shorts (cold water)

❐ Pump for inflatable SUP

❐ Two-way radios

❐ Warm cap (cold water)

❐ Waterproof camera

❐ Wetsuit (cold water)

SURFING

Essentials

- ❐ Board shorts or swimsuit
- ❐ Cell phone in protective case or waterproof smartwatch
- ❐ Clothing for water temperature (not air temperature)
- ❐ Compass that floats
- ❐ Deck bag or dry bags
- ❐ First-aid kit
- ❐ Flashlight, waterproof
- ❐ GPS
- ❐ Guidebook, maps, charts in waterproof case
- ❐ Healthy snacks and beverages
- ❐ Knife or multi-tool
- ❐ Lip balm
- ❐ Safety whistle
- ❐ Sun-protective shirt or rash guard
- ❐ Sunscreen
- ❐ Surf earplugs
- ❐ Surf fins
- ❐ Surf poncho
- ❐ Surf watch
- ❐ Surf wax and traction pad
- ❐ Surfboard
- ❐ Surfboard bag
- ❐ Surfboard leash
- ❐ Towel

THINGS TO BE HAPPY ABOUT OUTDOORS

- whale-watching
- tooting of gulls
- when the ocean seems lit from within
- tiny things in nature
- unspoiled shoreline

- Water bottle(s) or hydration reservoir/ waistpack

- Water shoes or sandals
- Weather radio

Extras

- Boots
- Emergency blanket
- Gloves
- Headlamp
- Insect repellent

- Neoprene top and shorts (for cold water)
- Warm cap (cold water)
- Warm socks (cold water)
- Waterproof camera
- Wetsuit (cold water)

STAND UP ON A SURFBOARD

- Position yourself on the board so that the nose of the board is level with or just above the water.
- Once the wave takes you, it is time to pop up.
- Push your chest up with your arms, then pop your front foot forward toward the middle of the board.
- Let go of the board sides (rails) and stand up.
- Keep your knees bent and your weight on your back leg.

SWIMMING

Essentials

- ❏ Earplugs
- ❏ First-aid kit
- ❏ Nose clips
- ❏ Personal flotation device (PFD)
- ❏ Snacks and food
- ❏ Swim bag or backpack
- ❏ Swim cap
- ❏ Swim goggles
- ❏ Swimwear
- ❏ Towels
- ❏ Water bottle
- ❏ Water shoes or sandals

SAVE SOMEONE FROM DROWNING

If you want to help someone who is in trouble in the water and you can reach the person with an object, do the following from out of the water:

- Brace yourself on a pool deck, pier surface, or shoreline.
- Reach out to the person using any object that extends your reach: a pole, oar, paddle, tree branch, belt, and so on.
- When the person grasps the object, slowly and carefully pull them to safety.
- Keep your body low and lean back to avoid being pulled into the water.

Extras

- ❐ Ankle bands
- ❐ Anti-chafing lube
- ❐ Arm floaties
- ❐ Fins
- ❐ Kickboard
- ❐ Mesh bag(s)
- ❐ Paddles
- ❐ Pool toys
- ❐ Pull buoy
- ❐ Resistance gloves
- ❐ Resistance pulley
- ❐ Swimming noodles
- ❐ Swimming paddles
- ❐ Swimming resistance bands
- ❐ Swimming rings
- ❐ Swimming shirt
- ❐ Swimming snorkel
- ❐ Wetsuit or speedsuit (cold water)

THINGS TO BE HAPPY ABOUT OUTDOORS

- soft, muted colors of seashells
- the sound of palm fronds
- lake water so clear you can see fish
- strands of seaweed
- a frog in the cattails

ULTIMATE FRISBEE

Essentials

❒ Appropriate clothes (jersey)

❒ Cleats

❒ Clothes for weather change

❒ Discs

❒ Food, snacks, beverages

❒ ID, keys, money

❒ Insect repellent

❒ Rainwear

❒ Sunglasses

❒ Sunscreen

❒ Towel

❒ Water bottle

DISPOSE OF WASTE PROPERLY

— For everything from litter to human waste to rinse water, pack it in and pack it out.
— Leave a place cleaner than you found it.
— Carry water 200 feet away from streams or lakes and use small amounts of biodegradable soap to wash yourself or dishes.
— Deposit solid human waste in cat holes dug 6 to 8 inches deep and at least 200 feet from water, campsites, and trails. Cover and disguise the cat hole when finished.
— Pack out toilet paper and hygiene products. Some areas require that human waste be packed out, too.

THINGS TO BE HAPPY ABOUT OUTDOORS

- the sky's colorful glow after sunset
- wild strawberries
- deep green shadows
- mist over a meadow
- bees rummaging in clover

Extras

- ❐ After-play shoes
- ❐ Cones
- ❐ Disc clip
- ❐ Gloves
- ❐ Hygiene supplies
- ❐ Leggings or tights
- ❐ Pads and braces
- ❐ Trash bag

URBAN HIKING

Essentials

- ❐ Cell phone or watch with GPS
- ❐ Daypack
- ❐ First-aid kit
- ❐ Gloves
- ❐ Hat
- ❐ Hiking or walking footwear
- ❐ Hiking poles or staff
- ❐ ID, keys, money
- ❐ Insect repellent or insect-repellent clothing
- ❐ Knife or multi-tool
- ❐ Food, snacks, beverages
- ❐ Sun protection
- ❐ Water bottle(s)
- ❐ Weather-appropriate active apparel

THINGS TO BE HAPPY ABOUT OUTDOORS

- raindrops changing shape as they fall
- sedimentary rock stripes
- aspens fluttering
- bunnies chomping roadside
- night sky stars

Extras

- ☐ Bandanna or buff
- ☐ Clothes for warmer and cooler conditions
- ☐ Extra clothes
- ☐ Rainwear

FOLLOW A BEARING

- — Hold your compass in front of you with the direction-of-travel arrow pointing in the direction you happen to be facing.
- — Walk around until the north end of the magnetic needle, which is usually red in color, coincides with the north arrow in the compass housing, usually marked with N.
- — Make sure it is your body that turns, not the compass baseplate.
- — Follow the direction-of-travel arrow toward your destination.
- — Periodically, recheck your bearing and recheck your location on a map.

WALKING, NORDIC WALKING

Essentials

- ❏ Cell phone or watch with GPS

- ❏ Daypack

- ❏ First-aid kit

- ❏ Gloves

- ❏ Hat

- ❏ ID, keys, money

- ❏ Insect repellent

- ❏ Knife or multi-tool

IMPROVISE A MAGNETIC COMPASS

- You'll need a 1- to 2-inch-long sewing needle, a small bar or refrigerator magnet, a small piece of cork, a shallow bowl, and pliers.
- Magnetize the needle by rubbing the magnet along it in one direction.
- Cut off a small circle at one end of the cork, about ¼-inch thick.
- Grip the needle with the pliers and, with the piece of cork on a flat surface, push the needle through it so it sticks out evenly from both sides of the cork.
- Fill the bowl halfway with water and put the cork-and-needle (compass) on the water.
- Watch the needle. It should point toward the nearest magnetic pole (north or south) depending on where you are.

- ☐ Lunch, snacks, beverages

- ☐ Rainwear

- ☐ Sun protection: sunglasses, sunscreen, lip balm

- ☐ Trekking or Nordic walking poles

- ☐ Walking footwear

- ☐ Water bottle(s)

- ☐ Weather-appropriate clothing (layers)

- ☐ Whistle

Extras

- ☐ After-walk shoes

- ☐ Bandanna or buff

- ☐ Clothes for warmer and cooler conditions

- ☐ Extra clothes and socks

- ☐ Handkerchief

WINDSURFING

Essentials

- ❏ Board bag
- ❏ Board shorts or swimsuit
- ❏ Buoyancy aid
- ❏ Cell phone in waterproof container or waterproof smartwatch
- ❏ Compass that floats
- ❏ Earplugs
- ❏ Eye protection
- ❏ Eyewear retainer
- ❏ Fins
- ❏ First-aid kit
- ❏ Gloves
- ❏ Harness
- ❏ Harness line
- ❏ Helmet
- ❏ Lip balm
- ❏ Personal flotation device (PFD)
- ❏ Rescue coat
- ❏ Roof rack for windsurfer
- ❏ Safety whistle
- ❏ Sun-protective shirt or rash guard
- ❏ Sunglasses and retainer strap
- ❏ Sunscreen
- ❏ Towel
- ❏ Water bottle(s) or hydration pack
- ❏ Weather radio
- ❏ Wetsuit

THINGS TO BE HAPPY ABOUT OUTDOORS

- soft, smooth beaches
- a nest of wet stones
- the food chain in action
- mandarin duck
- a turtle, sunning

- ❑ Windsurf rig: sail, mast, boom
- ❑ Windsurfing board
- ❑ Windsurfing insurance
- ❑ Windsurfing shoes or boots

Extras

- ❑ Emergency blanket
- ❑ Flashlight, waterproof
- ❑ GPS
- ❑ Headlamp
- ❑ Insect repellent
- ❑ Maps and charts in waterproof case
- ❑ Neoprene top and shorts (cold water)
- ❑ Two-way radios
- ❑ Warm cap (cold water)
- ❑ Waterproof camera
- ❑ Wetsuit (cold water)

MAKE A SUN COMPASS

— You need two straight sticks (one 3 feet long), a knife, and four small rocks (or substitute markers).
— Take the 3-foot-long stick and sharpen one end. Drive the stick into the ground in a flat, sunny spot.
— Mark the tip of the stick's shadow with a rock.
— Repeat the shadow-marking step every 15 minutes, three more times. You will have four points marked. Draw a line through the four points, creating your east–west line.
— Take the other (straight) stick and lay it at a right angle to the east–west line, pointing away from the long stick. This line points straight north (in the Northern Hemisphere).

ACTIVITIES

(defined as being more focused on nature, community or family-oriented)

1. Archaeology Dig

2. Beachcombing

3. Birding

4. Camping

5. Car Camping

6. Community Cleanup

7. Gardening, Landscaping

8. Geology Walk

9. Horse Riding

10. Nature Photography

11. Nature Walk

12. Spelunking, Caving

ETIQUETTE ON ARCHAEOLOGY DIG

- No obscene language or behavior.
- No sexual harassment.
- No threatening behavior or fighting.
- Address questions to your supervisor.
- Be courteous and enthusiastic toward visitors. If you are unsure about answering a question, refer the question to your supervisor.
- Be very careful around walls of and top edges of units.
- Develop good equipment habits. Clean items at the end of the day.
- Do not eat or drink in your unit.
- Do not presume that it is okay to step into someone else's unit.
- Keep meticulous records.
- Refrain from unnecessary jabber.
- Stay organized and keep your work area clean.

ARCHAEOLOGY DIG

Essentials

- ❏ Bandanna or buff
- ❏ Change-of-weather clothing
- ❏ Directions to site
- ❏ Field notebook with pen or pencil
- ❏ First-aid kit
- ❏ Flashlight
- ❏ Hand wipes
- ❏ Hat
- ❏ Hygiene items, such as deodorant
- ❏ Insect repellent
- ❏ Kneeling pad
- ❏ Lunch, snacks, beverages
- ❏ Multi-tool or knife
- ❏ Paper towels
- ❏ Permanent ink marker (like Sharpie)
- ❏ Rainwear
- ❏ Sunglasses
- ❏ Sunscreen
- ❏ Tissue pack(s)
- ❏ Towel
- ❏ Trowel(s)

- ☐ Wash-and-wear clothing (light-colored long-sleeve cotton work shirt, jeans or khaki pants)

- ☐ Water bottle(s)

- ☐ Work gloves

- ☐ Work shoes or boots (though heavy boots are not suitable for soft-floored sites)

Extras

- ☐ Blanket

- ☐ Blaze-orange clothing (if in the woods during hunting season or in a low-visibility or high-traffic area)

- ☐ Bungee cord

- ☐ Camp stool or chair

- ☐ Clipboard

- ☐ Collection bags

- ☐ Compass

- ☐ Dust pan and small whisk broom

- ☐ Extra clothes and socks

- ☐ Extra gloves

- ☐ Folding ruler

- ☐ Graph paper

- ☐ Hair ties

- ☐ Level

- ☐ Magnifying glass

- ☐ Map

- ☐ Multi-tool shovel

- ☐ Munsell chart

- ❏ Paintbrush
- ❏ Root cutters
- ❏ Shoes for after dig
- ❏ Tape (25 feet)
- ❏ Trash bags
- ❏ Whistle

THINGS TO BE HAPPY ABOUT OUTDOORS

- seeing life in soil layers
- the colors of the earth
- worms after a rain
- a bird's shadow whisking across the side of a building
- an ant's eye view

BEACHCOMBING

Essentials

- ❐ Appropriate shoes, such as water shoes
- ❐ Bag, disposable, for debris and trash
- ❐ Bags or totes for collecting, canvas and mesh
- ❐ Beach towel
- ❐ Camera
- ❐ Cell phone and backup charger
- ❐ Daypack, waterproof
- ❐ Flashlight
- ❐ Garden rake
- ❐ Garden trowel
- ❐ Hat or visor
- ❐ Layers of clothing, including jacket or sweatshirt
- ❐ Magnifying glass
- ❐ Pail
- ❐ Sand scoop
- ❐ Sand sifter
- ❐ Shell and rock field guide
- ❐ Sunglasses
- ❐ Sunscreen
- ❐ Tide chart
- ❐ Watch
- ❐ Water bottle

THINGS TO BE HAPPY ABOUT OUTDOORS

- treasure after a rainstorm
- something amazing created by nature
- the sloshing of ocean waves
- seagulls eyeing you
- the shoreline crumbled into fine grains

Extras

- ❏ Grabber
- ❏ Metal detector
- ❏ Putty knife
- ❏ Shovel

LEARN TO BEACHCOMB

- Check on the time of low tide. The best time to go beachcombing is 2 to 3 hours prior to low tide or an hour or so after.
- The action of storms will wash up fossils, bones, seaweed, and other interesting treasures from the ocean floor.
- Do not tamper with obviously dangerous items like fishhooks, metal canisters, and needles
- It is against the law to walk on the dunes, an important part of the beach ecosystem.
- Go slowly, be patient, and look carefully.
- When handling organisms, be gentle.
- Be moderate in how many non-living shells and organisms you take home.
- Each rock that you turn over is part of an ecosystem. A rock might be an essential part of an animal's home or protect animals from predators and the sun.
- Do not take animals out of their natural setting, especially from a tide pool.
- Take along a hefty canvas bag for marine debris to dispose of in a garbage can later.
- Most importantly, respect the area you are exploring.

BIRDING

Essentials

- ☐ Base layers
- ☐ Binoculars
- ☐ Birding vest
- ☐ Camera and case
- ☐ Cell phone with birding apps
- ☐ Daypack or birding pack
- ☐ Emergency blanket
- ☐ Field guide and checklist
- ☐ Field journal and life list, weatherproof
- ☐ First-aid kit
- ☐ Flashlight or headlamp with batteries and extra batteries
- ☐ Food and snacks
- ☐ GPS
- ☐ Hat
- ☐ Hiking stick
- ☐ Insect repellent, maybe insect-repellent clothing
- ☐ Insulation jacket
- ☐ Lightweight hiking boots, maybe waterproof
- ☐ Map and compass
- ☐ Mud boots
- ☐ Pen or pencil
- ☐ Personal medication
- ☐ Phone charger
- ☐ Pocketknife or multi-tool
- ☐ Rainwear
- ☐ Spotting scope
- ☐ Sunglasses
- ☐ Sunscreen

THINGS TO BE HAPPY ABOUT OUTDOORS

- a baby bird
- the eyes of birds
- an awesome nest
- a smooth brown rabbit
- delicious fragrances on a gentle breeze

BIRD IDENTIFICATION STEPS

— First judge the bird's size and shape.
— Then look for its main color pattern.
— Take note of its behavior.
— Factor in what habitat it is in.

❏ Water bottle(s)

❏ Water treatment system

❏ Weather- and activity-appropriate clothing

Extras

❏ Backyard feeder

❏ Extra binoculars

❏ Extra food and water

❏ Extra socks and shoes

❏ Fire-making supplies: disposable lighter, waterproof matches in container, firestarter

❏ Trash bag

CAMPING

Essentials

❏ Backpack

❏ Batteries and extra batteries for devices

❏ Bearproof storage or hang bag for food

❏ Blankets

❏ Camp chairs and table

❏ Camp pillows

❏ Camping kitchen gear

❏ Camping permits and/or reservations

❏ Cell phone and charger

❏ Clean-up supplies

❏ Clothing for weather and change of weather

❏ Clothing repair kit

❏ Compass

❏ Cooler and ice

❏ Daypack

❏ Duct tape

❏ Emergency shelter and blanket

❏ Extra clothing

❏ Firestarter, lighter, matches in waterproof container

❏ First-aid kit

❏ Flashlight, headlamp, lantern with new batteries

❏ Fleece jacket or pullover

❏ Food and drinks, extra supply of food (in bearproof container)

❏ Gloves

CAMPING KITCHEN

- 5-gallon water jug
- Aluminum foil
- Bearproof food container or hang bag
- Can, bottle, wine openers
- Charcoal and lighter fuel (if grilling)
- Coffee/tea pot or system
- Cooking utensils: kitchen knife, spatula, serving spoon, tongs, peeler, skewers
- Cooler and ice
- Cutting board(s)
- Dish soap, sponge, scraper
- Dish towels
- Dishwashing bins or collapsible sink
- Dutch oven
- Eating utensils
- Firewood and kindling (if allowed)
- Food storage bin(s)
- Grill rack
- Kitchen storage bin
- Large mixing bowl(s)
- Long-handled lighter or waterproof matches
- Measuring cups
- Paper towels
- Plates, bowls, cups, mugs
- Pot holders or hot pads
- Pots and pans
- Resealable zipper bags
- Trash bags
- Two-burner stove and windscreen

❒ GPS

❒ Hand sanitizer and wipes

❒ Hat for weather and change of weather

❒ ID, keys, money

❒ Insect repellent, netting, maybe insect-repellent clothing

❒ Insulated sit pad

❒ Itinerary left with friend and also under car seat

❒ Journal and pen or pencil

- ❏ Map or guidebook
- ❏ Multi-tool or pocketknife
- ❏ Notebook with pencil or pen
- ❏ Nylon cord or rope
- ❏ Personal hygiene kit
- ❏ Rainwear
- ❏ Reading material or games
- ❏ Resealable zipper bags
- ❏ Signaling mirror
- ❏ Sleeping bag and pads
- ❏ Stove and fuel
- ❏ Sun protection: sunglasses, sunscreen, lip balm
- ❏ Supportive footwear
- ❏ Tent and backpack repair kit
- ❏ Tent or other shelter, ground cloth, tarp, reflective blanket
- ❏ Toilet tissue (in a plastic bag)
- ❏ Towels and biodegradable soap
- ❏ Trash bags
- ❏ Water bottles or hydration pack

THINGS TO BE HAPPY ABOUT OUTDOORS

- sleeping outdoors, beyond the envelope of civilization
- a beaver swimming
- nature painting broad, colorful strokes
- lightning bugs flashing
- that special star you wish on

❏ Water treatment system

❏ Waterproof container(s)

❏ Weather radio

❏ Whistle

Extras

❏ Axe, saw, or hatchet

❏ Bandanna or buff

❏ Beach towels

❏ Binoculars

❏ Camera

❏ Hand and foot warmers

❏ Mosquito nets

❏ Satellite messenger and/or personal locator beacon

❏ Small broom

❏ Smartwatch

❏ Solar charger/panel for devices

❏ Solar shower

❏ Swimsuit

❏ Trekking poles or walking staff

❏ Two-way radios

❏ Winter attire: mittens, boots, snow pants, long underwear

CAR CAMPING

Essentials

- ❏ Backpack or daypack
- ❏ Batteries and extra batteries for devices
- ❏ Bearproof storage or hang bag for food
- ❏ Blankets
- ❏ Camp chairs and table
- ❏ Camp pillows
- ❏ Camping kitchen gear
- ❏ Camping permits and/or reservations
- ❏ Cell phone and charger
- ❏ Clean-up supplies
- ❏ Clothes for weather and change of weather
- ❏ Compass
- ❏ Cooler and ice
- ❏ Duct tape
- ❏ Emergency blanket

THINGS TO BE HAPPY ABOUT OUTDOORS

- a field lined with cedar and spruce
- tiny snails among blades of grass
- a motley of flowers
- trees sitting out rainy days without complaint
- the sweet pulse of crickets

ESCAPE A SINKING VEHICLE

- Stay as calm as possible; the first 30 to 120 seconds is crucial.
- Take off the seatbelt.
- Do not open a vehicle door to try to escape.
- Roll down or break a window. Keep a glass-breaking tool in your car.
- Escape through the window.
- Swim to the surface as quickly as possible.

❏ Extra clothes

❏ Firestarter, lighter, matches in waterproof container

❏ First-aid kit

❏ Flashlight, headlamp, lantern with new batteries

❏ Food and drinks, extra of both

❏ Gloves

❏ GPS

❏ Hand sanitizer and wipes

❏ Hat

❏ ID, keys, money

❏ Insect repellent

❏ Itinerary left with someone and also under vehicle seat

❏ Map or guidebook

❏ Multi-tool or pocketknife

❏ Notebook and pen or pencil

❏ Nylon cord or rope

❏ Personal hygiene kit

- ❏ Rainwear
- ❏ Repair kit
- ❏ Signaling mirror
- ❏ Sleeping bag and pad or air mattress and pump or sleeping cot
- ❏ Stove and fuel
- ❏ Sun protection: sunglasses, sunscreen, lip balm
- ❏ Supportive footwear
- ❏ Tarp, sun shade, or screen house
- ❏ Tent and backpack repair kit
- ❏ Tent and footprint or hammock with no-see-um net
- ❏ Towels and biodegradable soap
- ❏ Trash bags and resealable zipper bags
- ❏ Water bottles or hydration pack
- ❏ Water treatment system
- ❏ Whistle

Extras

- ❏ Axe, saw, or hatchet
- ❏ Bandanna or buff
- ❏ Beach towels
- ❏ Binoculars
- ❏ Camera with spare battery and memory card
- ❏ Hand and foot warmers
- ❏ Mosquito nets
- ❏ Reading material
- ❏ Satellite messenger and/or personal locator beacon
- ❏ Small broom

❏ Smartwatch

❏ Solar charger for devices

❏ Solar shower

❏ Swimsuit

❏ Travel games or cards

❏ Trekking poles or walking staff

❏ Two-way radios

❏ Weather radio

COMMUNITY CLEANUP

For example, beach cleanup, beautification project, environmental cleanup, flower planting incentive, river cleanup, trash and litter collection

Essentials

- ❏ Base layer
- ❏ Cell phone and charger
- ❏ Extra clothing, socks, shoes
- ❏ First-aid kit
- ❏ Gloves, work or garden
- ❏ Grabber
- ❏ Hat or cap
- ❏ ID, keys, money
- ❏ Insect repellent
- ❏ Long pants and long-sleeve shirt
- ❏ Outer layer, especially for weather changes
- ❏ Rainwear
- ❏ Snacks or lunch
- ❏ Sturdy (maybe waterproof) shoes or boots
- ❏ Sunglasses
- ❏ Sunscreen
- ❏ Trash bags
- ❏ Water bottle

THINGS TO BE HAPPY ABOUT OUTDOORS

- bees humming
- exhilarating gusts of wind
- the woodsy smell of violets
- urban owls
- a surprise in the garden

IN-VEHICLE CHECKLIST

- Brush for brushing off insects
- Cell phone charger
- Duct tape
- Emergency bivy or blanket
- Extra clothes, underwear, socks
- Extra shoes
- First-aid kit
- Flashlight with extra batteries
- Gloves
- Hand sanitizer and wipes
- Hat
- Itinerary of trip
- Jacket, sweatshirt, raincoat
- Jumper cables
- Multi-tool
- Paper towels
- Signaling flare and mirror
- Snow removal tool/brush
- Toilet paper and hygiene items
- Trash bags
- Umbrella
- Water and nonperishable snacks

Extras

❏ Backpack or daypack

❏ Camera

❏ Extra food, snacks, water

❏ Hand sanitizer and wipes

GARDENING, LANDSCAPING

Essentials

- ❏ Bucket or bag for tools
- ❏ Digging fork
- ❏ Flower bulbs
- ❏ Garden hoe
- ❏ Garden hose with adjustable nozzle
- ❏ Garden rake
- ❏ Garden scissors
- ❏ Gardening gloves
- ❏ Grass seed
- ❏ Hand pruner
- ❏ Hand rake
- ❏ Hand weeder
- ❏ Knee pads
- ❏ Kneeler
- ❏ Lawn mower
- ❏ Leaf rake
- ❏ Loppers
- ❏ Planting information
- ❏ Pruner, long-handled
- ❏ Pruning shears
- ❏ Seed packets
- ❏ Shovels, flat and round-headed
- ❏ Soil knife
- ❏ Spade
- ❏ Stool, small and folding
- ❏ Topsoil
- ❏ Trowel, hand
- ❏ Watering can
- ❏ Watering wand
- ❏ Weeder
- ❏ Wheelbarrow

THINGS TO BE HAPPY ABOUT OUTDOORS

- ladybugs and aphids
- the netherworld of spiders
- background sounds of nature
- dew hanging off leaf tips
- mushrooms popped up after a rain

IDENTIFY VENOMOUS INSECTS

- In general, avoid spiders, especially large ones like the brown recluse and black widow.
- Wasps, hornets, and yellow jackets are also best avoided.
- Before you sit down, always look for insects on the surface. Red fire ants can be a big problem if you sit where they are.
- Avoid centipedes. You can recognize them by their shape and multiple legs. Caterpillars may also be venomous.
- Horsefly and blackfly bites can be large and painful.
- Chiggers are tiny mite larvae that can leave toxins under your skin. You can avoid them the same way you avoid ticks: Wear long pants and sleeves, tuck pants into socks, and stay out of grass and away from vegetation.

Extras

- ❑ Annual seeds or plants
- ❑ Bow rake
- ❑ Hand saw
- ❑ Hand soil shovel
- ❑ Hose storage
- ❑ Japanese gardener's knife (hori-hori)
- ❑ Leaf blower
- ❑ Perennial seeds or plants
- ❑ Water breaker
- ❑ Weed trimmer
- ❑ Wildflower seeds

GEOLOGY WALK

Essentials

- ❒ Backpack or daypack
- ❒ Binoculars
- ❒ Camera
- ❒ Cell phone and charger
- ❒ Compass
- ❒ Duct tape
- ❒ Field notebook and pen or pencil
- ❒ Field pants or shorts and field shirt
- ❒ First-aid kit
- ❒ Flashlight or headlamp (for night walk)
- ❒ Food, snacks, beverages
- ❒ Gloves
- ❒ Rock pick or hammer
- ❒ Specimen bags
- ❒ GPS
- ❒ Hand sanitizer
- ❒ Hat or cap
- ❒ ID, keys, money
- ❒ Insect repellent, maybe insect-repellent clothing
- ❒ Magnifying glass
- ❒ Map, topographic
- ❒ Outer layer for weather and change of weather
- ❒ Pocketknife or multi-tool
- ❒ Rainwear
- ❒ Rock and mineral field guide
- ❒ Rock and mineral list for the area

THINGS TO BE HAPPY ABOUT OUTDOORS

- heart-shaped pebbles
- cornfields rustling
- patterns in nature
- the way chipmunks move
- the undersides of rocks

- ❐ Sturdy (maybe waterproof) walking shoes or boots
- ❐ Sunglasses
- ❐ Sunscreen
- ❐ Water bottle
- ❐ Weather-appropriate clothing

Extras

- ❐ Extra clothing, socks, shoes
- ❐ Hiking stick
- ❐ Long pants and long-sleeve shirt
- ❐ Mud or snow boots
- ❐ Personal medications
- ❐ Trash bag
- ❐ Water treatment system

WARN ANIMALS YOU ARE THERE

— Remember that humans are taller, heavier, and noisier than 99 percent of the animals you will meet outside—and all other wildlife are scared of humans. Most animals will actively avoid you. But making noise and having loud conversations or singing will warn animals you are coming, so they can move to a quieter place.

— Stay a minimum of 100 yards from wildlife. If you unexpectedly are closer and an animal reacts to your presence—you are too close. You want to let wildlife be wild and observe from a distance.

— The only way animals will know you are nearby is through noise. Watch for animal tracks and poop.

— Make noise while you hike to avoid surprising a bear or other potentially threatening animal. You can shout, "Hey bear!" every few minutes, talk or sing loudly with fellow hikers, clap your hands, or strike trekking poles together.

— Some people wear bear bells or attach them to trekking poles. They need to be loud enough to be useful.

HORSE RIDING

Essentials

❐ Boots, tall or paddock boots

❐ Bridle and reins

❐ Cell phone charger

❐ Cell phone with GPS

❐ First-aid kit

❐ Fly spray

❐ Girth

❐ Gloves

❐ Halter and lead rope

❐ Harness

❐ Hat

❐ Helmet, riding

❐ Hoof pick

❐ Horse bit

❐ Horse grooming tools and supplies

❐ Horse treats

❐ ID, keys, money

❐ Insect repellent and fly mask

❐ Map of area/trail and compass

❐ Outerwear

❐ Pocketknife or multi-tool

READ ANIMAL TRACKS AND SCAT

- If you want to avoid crossing paths with unfriendly creatures, keep an eye out for unique scat and tracks.
- Rodents' pellets look like pencil lead, and the tracks are two small prints just above two larger ones, fairly close together.
- Rabbits and hares leave small, circular pellets like M&M candies. Their tracks are two small prints above two larger ones that are farther apart.
- The deer family leaves oval/oblong scat with a pointed end and hoof mark tracks.
- The dog family, including coyotes, leaves tubelike scat with tapered ends. You'll likely recognize the paw print for its four toes (often with claw imprint) and small back pad. Raccoons, skunks, opossums, and wolverines also leave tubular scat.
- The cat family, including cougars/mountain lions and bobcats, leaves teardrop or tapered scat and the paw print of four large toes and large back pad.
- Foxes have scat that is tubular and tapered at both ends (between a dog and cat). The tracks include claw marks, four toe pads, and a palm pad and are mostly oval.
- Birds of prey leave pellets with bone and hair. The tracks are three pronged.
- Bears leave tubular scat with hair, bone and fibers, or globular scat with berries, seeds, and vegetation. Bear tracks are broad—4 to 7 inches long—and often all five toes and claw marks show. The hind tracks are triangular. The largest toe mark is on the outside.

❑ Rainwear

❑ Riding boots or mud shoes

❑ Riding pants or jeans

❑ Saddle

❑ Saddle pad/blanket

❑ Snacks and food

❑ Stirrups

❑ Sunglasses

❑ Sunscreen

❑ Water bottle

Extras

❑ Breastplate

❑ Camera

❑ Extra food and snacks

❑ Extra gloves

❑ Extra socks

❏ Martingale

❏ Safety vest

❏ Shoes for after riding

❏ Toilet paper or urinary products

❏ Trip itinerary left with someone and also under vehicle seat

NATURE PHOTOGRAPHY

Essentials

- ❑ Appropriate outdoor clothing
- ❑ Bean bag support
- ❑ Binoculars or monocular
- ❑ Camera
- ❑ Camera backpack
- ❑ Camera case
- ❑ Cell phone and charger
- ❑ Cleaning kit and tools
- ❑ Clothing for weather change
- ❑ Extender/teleconverter
- ❑ Gimbal head
- ❑ Ground pod
- ❑ Hat or cap
- ❑ Headlamp

ORIENT TO THE NORTH STAR

- — Find the Big Dipper, an easy-to-identify group of seven stars.
- — Next find the "pointer" stars, the two stars that a liquid would run off if you tipped up the pan of the Big Dipper.
- — The North Star will always be five times the distance between these two pointers in the direction that they point (up away from the pan).
- — True north lies directly under this star.

- ❏ Lenses for nature photography
- ❏ Lighting equipment
- ❏ Long lens rain cover
- ❏ Rainwear
- ❏ Telephoto-zoom lens
- ❏ Tripod
- ❏ Wide-angle lens

Extras

- ❏ Ball head
- ❏ Bracket
- ❏ Extra camera and camera supplies
- ❏ Extra socks and shoes
- ❏ Filters
- ❏ Flashes
- ❏ Hand and foot warmers
- ❏ Photography apps
- ❏ Remote cable shutter release
- ❏ Towel

THINGS TO BE HAPPY ABOUT OUTDOORS

- birds through the viewfinder
- catching the first flower to bloom in your yard
- a nest filled with eggs
- nature's details seen in bright sunshine
- an animal peering from a hole

NATURE WALK

Essentials

- ❑ Backpack or daypack
- ❑ Binoculars
- ❑ Camera
- ❑ Cell phone and charger
- ❑ Field guide
- ❑ First-aid kit
- ❑ Flashlight or headlamp (for night walk)
- ❑ Food and snacks
- ❑ Gloves
- ❑ Hand sanitizer

MARK YOUR TRAIL

- If you want others to be able to follow your path in the outdoors, use these international trailblazing symbols using grass, sticks, or rocks—whatever is handy.
- Three of anything—sticks lined up parallel or three large rocks stacked—indicates danger.
- Two items crossed indicates "not the way."
- To indicate turn left, put a single rock on the left and two on the right (next to each other). If you use sticks, the left one is straight and the right one leans left and connects at the top of the left stick. It is like the beginning of the capital letter N.
- To indicate turn right, put a single rock on the right and two on the left (next to each other). If you use sticks, the right one is straight and the left one leans right and connects at the top of the right stick.
- To direct someone to "head this way," put a large rock on the bottom and a smaller one on top of it. Using sticks, one stands up straight and another connects to it at the bottom and is pointed in the direction to head.

THINGS TO BE HAPPY ABOUT OUTDOORS

- gentle steps on the earth
- foam dissolving as waves recede
- deeply grooved bark
- your mind under nature's influence
- inhaling the smells of the day

- ❏ Hat or cap
- ❏ ID, keys, money
- ❏ Insect repellent
- ❏ Magnifying glass
- ❏ Map and compass or GPS
- ❏ Nature journal and pen or pencil
- ❏ Outer layer for weather and change of weather
- ❏ Pocketknife or multi-tool

- ❏ Rainwear
- ❏ Specimen bag
- ❏ Sturdy (maybe waterproof) walking shoes or boots
- ❏ Sunglasses
- ❏ Sunscreen
- ❏ Water bottle
- ❏ Weather-appropriate clothing

Extras

- ❏ Extra clothing, socks, shoes
- ❏ Hiking stick
- ❏ Long pants and long-sleeve shirt

- ❏ Mud or snow boots
- ❏ Trash bag
- ❏ Water treatment system

SPELUNKING, CAVING

Essentials

- ❏ Backpack, waterproof
- ❏ Batteries and extra batteries for devices
- ❏ Camera
- ❏ Candles (6-hour) and waterproof matches
- ❏ Cave directions and description
- ❏ Caving pack
- ❏ Cell phone in protective case
- ❏ Chemical light stick
- ❏ Clothing (in layers)
- ❏ Compass
- ❏ Coveralls or overalls or caving suit
- ❏ Dry bags
- ❏ Duct tape
- ❏ Elbow pads
- ❏ Emergency phone numbers
- ❏ First-aid kit
- ❏ Flashlight and spare
- ❏ Food and snacks

NAVIGATE WITH A WATCH

- A watch can be used to help you navigate if you do not have a compass.
- For Northern Hemisphere temperate zones, lay the watch horizontally and line up the sun with your watch's hour hand. The midpoint between the sun and the twelve o'clock marker is the north–south divide. The point closest to the sun will be south. The point opposite it will be north.
- For the Southern Hemisphere temperate zones, lay the watch horizontally and line up the sun with the twelve o'clock position. Imagine a line bisecting the space between the twelve o'clock position and the hour hand; this will be north. The opposite will be south.

- ❏ Gloves
- ❏ GPS
- ❏ Hand-line and carabiner
- ❏ Headlamp
- ❏ Heat packs
- ❏ Helmet with headlamp and alternate light source
- ❏ Hiking boots and high-quality socks
- ❏ Insect repellent
- ❏ Knee pads
- ❏ Long underwear
- ❏ Map of cave
- ❏ Multi-tool or pocketknife
- ❏ Notebook, with waterproof paper, and pencils
- ❏ Personal locator beacon
- ❏ Resealable zipper bags
- ❏ Towel(s)
- ❏ Trash bag
- ❏ Watch
- ❏ Water

Extras

- ❏ Dry clothes for afterward
- ❏ Extra clothing and hat (water-sealed)
- ❏ Extra food and water
- ❏ Extra gloves
- ❏ FRS (Family Radio Service) radio
- ❏ Spare headlamp
- ❏ Sunglasses
- ❏ Toilet paper

BE BEAR AWARE

— If camping, pitch your camp in a quiet, open area where you'll be visible to wildlife and wildlife will be visible to you. Suspend food out of reach in a hanging sack, or use a bearproof canister. Do not leave any food in or near your tent. Do your cooking at least 100 feet downwind from the campsite.

— If you see a bear before it sees you, back away slowly, keeping an eye on the bear. Retreat or reroute to give the bear a wide berth.

— If you have bear spray, get it ready.

— If you see a brown/grizzly bear, stay calm, back up slowly, and do *not* make eye contact. Talk in a friendly tone. Grab your bear spray, but do not turn and run. Back up, whether the bear retreats or keeps coming.

— If a grizzly bear attacks, play dead if you do not have bear spray. Stay flat on your stomach, putting your backpack between you and the bear. Cover the back of your neck with your hands.

— If a black bear is coming toward you, make a lot of noise and make yourself look bigger. Throw objects to scare it off.

— If threatened by a black bear, do not climb a tree, as it can climb it, too. Stand still if charged; the bear may be bluffing. If attacked by a black bear, fight back using anything you're carrying or can pick up.

SAFETY

FIRST AID

There are premade first-aid kits, which most
people use instead of buying individual supplies
and assembling a kit. When buying a kit,
consider the number of people the kit will serve
(is it usually a twosome? a whole family?), the
trip length/distance, and the trip activity or
activities. A premade kit usually lists the number of people it
serves and the estimated number of days it covers. If your plans
involve water, you should look for a waterproof pouch. You may
need a smaller and lighter kit for something like trail running, or
a larger kit for camping.

You should also consider the risks on the trip and any special
needs for yourself and others. It might be smart to own multiple
kits for your various activities. And make sure that the kit is in
your vehicle before you head out.

First-Aid Kit Essentials

☐ acetaminophen, ibuprofen, or aspirin

☐ adhesive and butterfly bandages, assorted

☐ adhesive tape

☐ antacid tablets

☐ antibiotic ointment

☐ antihistamine cream

☐ antiseptic ointment

☐ antiseptic soap

☐ antiseptic towelettes/wet wipes

☐ blister plasters, moleskin, treatments

☐ burn ointment, dressing

☐ chemical cold and heat packs

☐ cotton balls/cotton swabs

☐ diarrhea medicine

- ❏ duct tape
- ❏ elastic wrap/Ace bandage
- ❏ EpiPens and antihistamine tablets
- ❏ facial tissue packages
- ❏ first-aid instructions
- ❏ gauze roll and/or pads
- ❏ hydrocortisone cream
- ❏ hydrogen peroxide
- ❏ matches
- ❏ mild laxative
- ❏ mild sedative
- ❏ mirror, small and unbreakable
- ❏ personal prescription medicines
- ❏ poison-ivy medication
- ❏ razor blade (safety) or knife
- ❏ rubbing alcohol or alcohol swabs
- ❏ safety pins
- ❏ salt tablets or electrolyte powders
- ❏ scissors (blunt tip) or Swiss Army knife with scissors
- ❏ smelling salts
- ❏ sterile gauze pads, two sizes
- ❏ sugar packets and salt packets or rehydration salts
- ❏ tweezers/tick remover, needle and thread
- ❏ water purification tablets

First-Aid Kit Extras

- ❏ bee-sting kit
- ❏ bulb-irrigating syringe

- ❏ cell phone

- ❏ ground sheet

- ❏ insect repellent

- ❏ medication alert

- ❏ motion-sickness medication

- ❏ paper cups and plastic spoons

- ❏ sheet, towels, blanket

- ❏ snakebite kit (freeze kit)

- ❏ splints

- ❏ sunscreen

- ❏ tourniquet

First-Aid Instructions

This information is not intended as a substitute for professional medical advice, emergency treatment, or formal first-aid training. Don't use this information to diagnose or develop a treatment plan for a health problem or disease without consulting a qualified health-care provider. If you're in a life-threatening or emergency medical situation, seek medical assistance immediately.

FIRST-AID LIFESAVING SEQUENCE

Evaluation:

- Size up the scene.

- Identify life threats.

- Do a focused exam: head-to-toe check, vital signs, and patient history.

- Make a problem list and care plan, which includes an evacuation decision.

- Treat the patient, providing both medical and emotional support.

- Monitor how the patient is doing.

Preparation:

- Determine whether the area is safe: Ensure no further harm is imminent—for both patient and responders. If a rockslide caused the injury, for example, you might need to move the patient out of the path of additional rockfall.

- Identify the mechanism of injury (MOI). Look around to determine what might have caused the accident or injury. This provides clues to the type of injuries that might be present.

- Form a general impression of the seriousness of the situation. If the patient is injured, how injured? If the person is sick, how sick?

- Determine the number of patients. Don't assume that the most obviously injured person is the only one in need of assessment and care.

- Protect yourself: Prudent caregiver practice is to assume all people are infectious. Put on gloves and a mask, and wash hands thoroughly before and after patient contact.

INITIAL PATIENT ASSESSMENT

- Obtain consent to treat (if the person is conscious). Ask the person if you can help. If the answer is "yes," then ask their name, symptoms, and what happened.

- Establish responsiveness. Attempt to wake the patient if they aren't responding. (If there is any possibility of a spine injury, you also need to carefully place your hands on either side of the person's head and keep the patient still.)

- Airway check: Look in the mouth and check the airway for obstructions.

- Breathing check: Look closely at the chest; listen and feel for signs of respiration.

- Circulation check: Check for a pulse and for major wounds that are bleeding.

- Disability decision: If you can't rule out a spine injury, continue to protect it.

- Expose injuries: Without moving the patient, open up clothing covering serious injuries so you can fully evaluate and treat them.

SECONDARY PATIENT ASSESSMENT

Head-to-Toe Exam:

- Look: for blood and other bodily fluids, discoloration, or unusual shapes.

- Listen: for airway noises or unusual sounds when joints are moved.

- Feel: for wounds, deformities and unexpected hardness, softness, or tenderness.

- Smell: for unusual odors.

- Ask: if anything hurts or feels odd or numb.

Check Vital Signs:

- Level of responsiveness: Is the patient awake and oriented? Awake and disoriented? Or unconscious or unresponsive?

- Heart rate: Using the wrist pulse, check the number of beats per minute and note whether the pulse is strong or weak, regular or irregular.

- Respiration rate: Check the patient's number of breaths per minute and note whether the breathing is easy or labored.

- Skin signs: Look at skin color, temperature, and moisture. The inside rim of the lower eye or inside the lower lip are good places to check for color. Is it pink or pale? Is the rest of their skin warm and dry vs. cool and clammy? If possible, also record the patient's temperature with a thermometer.

Do a Patient History:

- Chief complaint: Ask the following questions: What is your most significant concern? When did it start? What makes it worse or better? Where is it located? How severe is it?

- How old is the patient?

- Symptoms: Ask if the patient can provide additional details about the chief complaint, or if they have other conditions or concerns.

- Allergies: Are there severe ones? (Food and medicine are common ones; also ask about bees.) What are the patient's reactions to their allergies?

- Medications: Get as many details as possible for both prescription and over-the-counter drugs.

- Pertinent medical history: Find out if they have any medical conditions that require them to see a doctor for treatment.

- Last fluid/food intake, last urine/bowel output: How long ago and how much?

- Events: Ask if they know what caused the event and the details leading up to it.

Tips:

- If possible, have someone of the same gender perform the head-to-toe exam.

- Have someone help the examiner by writing down observations and vital signs.

- Assign other tasks, like boiling water for drinks or setting up camp, so that the patient feels like care is orderly and all rescuers have a role.

- Try to keep the patient clean, warm, and comfortable at all times. If you are waiting for help to arrive, things like shelter, sustenance, and general nursing care will be key to maintaining patient well-being.

- Fluids are more important than food; avoid caffeinated and sugary drinks.

- Offer emotional support and empathy.

- Inform the patient about all aspects of care and involve them in evacuation decisions.

- Resupply and/or supplement your first-aid kit before each trip (consider a larger tube of antibiotic ointment or more dressing materials, among other things).

ALLERGIC REACTION, MILD

- Take an antihistamine such as Benadryl.

- Avoid scratching, as this will further irritate the rash, increase the risk of infection, and cause scarring.

- Apply cornstarch packs to reduce the itching of hives.

- Apply a thin layer of steroid cream, such as hydrocortisone, to rashes caused by allergens rubbed against the skin.

- Apply calamine lotion to poison oak and insect bites. Steroid cream may also be effective with poison oak.

ALLERGIC REACTION, SEVERE

- Know in advance what your companions are allergic to and where they keep their inhalers, epinephrine kits, and allergy medications. Consider wearing a medic alert bracelet if you know you are susceptible to anaphylactic shock.

- Learn to identify the signs and symptoms of anaphylaxis: difficulty breathing, wheezing, rash, itching, hives, swelling of the feet, hands, eyes, or face, flushed skin, nausea, vomiting, abdominal pain, rapid pulse.

- Remove the person from contact with the allergen if the allergen is suspected to be something in the air or on the skin.

- Administer injectable epinephrine (adrenaline) immediately if the person is having difficulty talking or breathing. Epinephrine is usually prescribed in an Anakit or EpiPen with a preloaded syringe, and is injected intramuscularly in the thigh for rapid absorption.

- Monitor airway, breathing, and circulation.

- Treat for shock.

- Inject a second dose of epinephrine within 12 to 15 minutes after the first dose was administered to prevent a relapse. Most kits contain at least two doses.

- Administer an oral antihistamine once the epinephrine has taken effect and the person is able to take the medication on their own.

- Hydrate well.
- Evacuate immediately, administering oral antihistamines at regular intervals until the person has reached professional medical care.

BANDAGING A WOUND

- Protect yourself. Scrub your hands thoroughly with soap and disinfected water, and put on medical gloves to prevent the spread of infectious disease.
- Clean the wound and carefully remove any excess debris.
- Remove any jewelry, such as rings or watches, that might impair circulation.
- Apply antibiotic cream to the inside of the material you are using as a dressing.
- Cover the wound with the dressing. The dressing should extend beyond the wound by about ½ inch so that it covers the wound completely and allows room to affix the dressing to uninjured skin.
- Cut four strips of adhesive tape and affix them to the dressing and skin on all four sides of the dressing. The purpose of the bandage is to help keep the dressing in place, and it shouldn't be too loose (able to move around) or too tight (impairing circulation).
- If there is a risk that the wound will be exposed to water, cover the bandage with waterproof material such as waterproof tape or plastic.
- Look at and feel the area and limb surrounding the wound to make certain the dressing does not impair circulation.
- Ask the injured person if they can feel the area you are touching, feel no pain or tingling, and can move the limb fully. The skin should be pink and slightly warm to the touch.

BITE FROM ANIMAL

- Move away from the animal and ensure the safety of the scene to prevent additional bites.

- Put on medical gloves as protection from infectious disease.
- Clean the wound thoroughly and aggressively with an antiseptic soap or povidone-iodine solution.
- Keep the wound open—do not attempt to close it with closure strips or butterfly bandages.
- Dress and bandage the wound.
- Keep the patient well-hydrated.
- Monitor carefully for infection.
- Evacuate immediately to a hospital, regardless of whether or not you believe the animal was rabid.

BITE FROM INSECT

- Wash the area with soap and water.
- Apply a cool compress to help reduce pain and swelling. Use a cloth dampened with cold water or filled with ice. If the injury is on an arm or leg, elevate it.
- Apply 0.5 or 1 percent hydrocortisone cream, calamine lotion, or a baking soda paste to the bite or sting several times daily until symptoms go away.
- Take an antihistamine (Benadryl, others) to reduce itching.
- If the signs and symptoms do not disappear in a few days or if you are concerned, get medical help.

BITE FROM SNAKE

- Move away from the snake and ensure safety of the scene to prevent additional bites.
- Calm the patient down and keep them still and quiet.
- Elevate the bite at or below the level of the heart.
- Remove any jewelry or other articles that may constrict with swelling.
- Suction immediately with a Sawyer Extractor, ideally within 3 minutes after the patient has been bit.

- If extractor not available: Apply hard direct pressure over bite using a 4 x 4 gauze pad folded in half twice. Soak gauze pad in antiseptic soap or solution if available. Strap gauze pad tightly in place with adhesive tape.

- Overwrap dressing above and below bite area with an Ace or crepe bandage, but not too tightly—no tighter than you would use for a sprain. Check for pulse above and below elastic wrap; if absent it is too tight. Unpin and loosen.

- Immobilize the extremity, and splint if possible.

- Keep the patient well-hydrated.

- Evacuate immediately, preferably without any effort on the part of the patient. An ideal evacuation would involve sending others to arrange for a helicopter evacuation. Get the patient to the hospital immediately.

BITE FROM SPIDER

- Clean the wound. Use mild soap and water and apply an antibiotic ointment.

- Apply a cool compress to help reduce pain and swelling. Use a cloth dampened with cold water or filled with ice. If the bite is on an arm or leg, elevate it.

- Take an over-the-counter pain medication if needed. If the wound is itchy, an antihistamine (Benadryl, Chlor-Trimeton, or similar) may help.

BLEEDING, STOPPING

- Elevate the injured area above the heart.

- Apply direct pressure to the bleeding area, using sterile cloth or gauze.

- Keep the pressure on for 5 minutes.

- Check to see if the bleeding has stopped. If it hasn't, apply pressure for 15 minutes.

BLISTER

- Try to keep a blister intact by covering it with a bandage or using a piece of moleskin cut into a doughnut shape to encircle the blister and give it air.

- Seek medical care if a blister looks infected.

BURN

- Remove the source of the burn: For flame burns, stop, drop, and roll; for wet chemical burns, flush the area with water for 20 minutes; for dry chemical burns, brush off the dry chemicals.

- Remove any clothing and jewelry, since they retain heat and can exacerbate burning.

- Check airway, breathing, and circulation. Treat with rescue breathing and/or CPR as necessary.

- Cool the burn with cold (but warmer than ice-cold) water, or with cloths dampened with cold water.

- Assess the depth and extent of the burn.

- Elevate the burn site above the heart.

- Have the injured person drink as much as possible, unless they are unconscious and/or showing signs of shock.

- Clean the burn area gently with disinfected lukewarm water and mild soap. Pat dry, then flush any debris out with an irrigation syringe. Pat dry again.

- Apply a thin layer of antibiotic ointment to the burn site with a cotton swab.

- Cover the burn with dry, sterile gauze.

- Give ibuprofen to reduce pain and swelling.

- Evacuate unless only minor superficial burns are involved.

- Re-dress the burn twice a day on the hike out: Remove the dressing (which may require soaking it first), rewash the burn site, reapply antibiotic ointment, and re-dress with gauze.

CLEANING A WOUND

- Scrub hands thoroughly with soap and disinfected water.

- Put on medical gloves to prevent the spread of infectious disease.

- Prepare a disinfectant solution of 1 ounce povidone-iodine and 1 liter disinfected water.

- Set the disinfectant solution aside for about 5 minutes.

CPR

- Determine if the surrounding scene is safe.

- If not in a wilderness setting, tell someone nearby to call 911.

- Determine if the injured person is breathing.

- Position the injured person on their back, being extremely careful not to move or twist the head, neck, or spine. If several rescuers are present, use their assistance to minimize this danger.

- Maintain an open airway while you pinch the injured person's nose shut.

- Give two long, slow breaths, being sure to maintain a seal between your mouth and the patient's mouth.

- Begin CPR if the person is neither breathing nor has a pulse.

- Position the hands: Find the lower tip of the breastbone. Measure two finger widths toward the head, and place the heel of one hand in this location.

- Place your other hand on top of the first hand, interlacing the fingers of both hands.

- Lean forward so that your shoulders are over your hands.

- Push downward on the chest, using the weight of your upper body for strength. Compress fifteen times in 10 seconds.

- Give two more slow breaths after the fifteen compressions.

- Do fifteen more compressions followed again by two slow breaths.

- Perform the fifteen-compression/two-breath cycle a total of four times.

- Recheck for pulse and breathing.

- Continue repeating this entire cycle—four sets of chest compressions and breaths followed by rechecking pulse and breathing—until the injured person regains a pulse, professional medical help arrives, or you are too exhausted to continue.

CRAMP

- Move the person out of direct sunlight, preferably into a cool, shaded area.

- Stretch the calf and thigh muscles gently through the cramp. This will usually bring immediate relief.

- Hydrate well, preferably with a diluted sports drink or oral rehydration solution. A teaspoon of salt in a liter of water will also work.

- Have the person rest quietly.

FROSTBITE, MILD

- Consider taking a pain reliever such as ibuprofen to brace for the inevitable pain of rewarming.

- Gather the following supplies if possible: a camp stove with fuel, a pot in which to heat water, a receptacle large enough to hold the affected body part without allowing it to touch the sides, and a thermometer to check the water's temperature.

- Heat the right amount of water—enough to cover the affected area once it's in the receptacle—to between 104 and 108 degrees F.

- Pour the heated water into the receptacle.

- Immerse the affected part—stripped of all clothing and covering—in the water, taking care that it doesn't touch the sides of the receptacle.

- Heat more water, again to between 104 and 108 degrees F.

- Replace the water in the receptacle once it has cooled to below 100 degrees F.

- Repeat the heat-and-replace cycle until all discoloration has disappeared and the tissue is once again soft and pliable. This usually takes 30 to 60 minutes.

- Prepare a bath of water mixed with antibacterial soap. Immerse the affected area for 5 minutes to minimize risk of infection.

- Air-dry the injured area and gingerly apply aloe vera ointment.

- Cover the injured area gently with dry sterile gauze and insulating layers.

- Evacuate if you are outdoors, taking extreme care not to let the frostbitten body part refreeze.

FROSTBITE, SEVERE

- Figure out if it's possible to evacuate without the affected area being used. For instance, can the person be moved without walking on a frostbitten foot?

- Decide if you'll be able to keep the person, including the affected area, warm throughout the eventual evacuation.

- Determine if you have all the supplies for field rewarming: the ability to heat a lot of water for a long time, a receptacle large enough to hold the affected part without allowing it to touch the sides, and a thermometer to check the water's temperature.

- Rewarm in the field only if the above three conditions are met: no necessity to use the affected area before reaching a hospital, ability to keep the person warm during the evacuation, and adequate supplies to rewarm properly. Otherwise, evacuate before rewarming.

HEAT EXHAUSTION

Evaluate for heat exhaustion. If you suspect heat exhaustion, treat with the following steps:

- Move the person out of direct sunlight, preferably into a cool, shaded area.

- If the person feels dizzy or has fainted suddenly, have them lie flat and elevate their feet.

- Have the person rest quietly.

- Move to a cool, shaded area.

- Hydrate well with lots of water or a diluted sports drink or oral rehydration solution.

- Remove heat-retaining clothing.

- Wet the person down and fan them with a shirt or towel.

- Place a wet bandanna or thin strip of cotton cloth on the person's forehead, top of the head, or back of the neck.

- Monitor body temperature frequently. If it rises to above 104 degrees, aggressively cool the person.

HEATSTROKE

Evaluate for heatstroke. Warning signs vary but may include high temperature (over 103 degrees), red-hot dry skin with no sweating, rapid strong pulse, throbbing headache, dizziness, nausea, confusion, and unconsciousness. If you suspect heatstroke, treat with the following steps:

- Move the patient out of direct sunlight, preferably into a cool, shaded area.

- Have the patient lie flat and elevate their feet.

- Remove heat-retaining clothing.

- Wet the patient down and fan them, or immerse the patient in cool water.

- Place ice packs on the patient's head, back of the neck, armpits, palms of the hands or soles of the feet, and groin.

- Hydrate well with lots of water or a diluted sports drink or oral rehydration solution, but only if the patient is conscious enough to hold a cup and drink unassisted.

- Monitor body temperature frequently, keeping careful notes on how long the patient remains at a given temperature. Transfer these notes when you transfer care.

- Evacuate immediately, continually monitoring and writing down the patient's body temperature.

HEIMLICH MANEUVER

The Heimlich maneuver is an emergency procedure to help someone who is choking because food is lodged in the trachea. To perform abdominal thrusts (Heimlich maneuver) on someone else:

- Stand behind the person. Place one foot slightly in front of the other for balance. Wrap your arms around their waist. Tip the person forward slightly. If a child is choking, kneel down behind the child.

- Make a fist with one hand. Position it slightly above the person's navel.

- Grasp the fist with the other hand. Press hard into the abdomen with a quick, upward thrust—as if trying to lift the person up.

- Perform between six and ten abdominal thrusts until the blockage is dislodged.

HYPOTHERMIA, MILD

- Remove the affected person from the cold, wet, and/or windy environment.

- Dry the person off, replacing wet clothing with dry clothing.

- Shelter the person however possible: in a cave, under an overhang, in an improvised shelter such as a tent or under a rain fly.

- Make sure the person is wearing a dry hat: A large percentage of body-heat loss occurs through the head.

- Cover their neck with something dry: A lot of heat is also lost through the neck.

- If you have a camp stove, prepare a warm (not hot) beverage and have the hypothermic person drink it.

- Encourage the person to eat carbohydrate-rich foods.
- Encourage the person to move around, which generates heat and helps with rewarming.

HYPOTHERMIA, MODERATE

- Remove the affected person from the cold, wet, and/or windy environment.
- Dry the person off, replacing wet clothing with dry clothing.
- Shelter the person however possible: in a cave, under an overhang, in an improvised shelter such as a tent or under a rain fly.
- Make sure the person is wearing a dry hat: A large percentage of body-heat loss occurs through the head.
- Cover their neck with something dry: A lot of heat is also lost through the neck.
- Insulate the person from the ground and the surrounding cold by having them lie in a sleeping bag on a sleeping pad.
- If you have a camp stove, prepare a warm (not hot) beverage and have the hypothermic person drink it.
- Encourage the person to eat carbohydrate-rich foods.
- Place hot water bottles (filled with hot water) and/or chemical heat packs inside the sleeping bag and against the clothing of the hypothermic person.
- Build a fire near the person, but take care that it isn't close enough to risk catching anything on fire.
- Monitor closely for changes in level of consciousness: A worsening condition may indicate severe hypothermia.

HYPOTHERMIA, SEVERE

- Remove the affected person from the cold, wet, and/or windy environment.
- Dry the person off, replacing wet clothing with dry clothing.

- Shelter the person however possible: in a cave, under an overhang, in an improvised shelter such as a tent or under a rain fly.
- Make sure the person is wearing a dry hat: A large percentage of body-heat loss occurs through the head.
- Cover their neck with something dry: A lot of heat is also lost through the neck.
- Insulate the person from the ground and the surrounding cold by having them lie in a sleeping bag on a sleeping pad.
- Place hot water bottles (filled with hot water) and/or chemical heat packs inside the sleeping bag and against the clothing of the hypothermic person.
- Build a "hypothermia wrap" by placing dry clothing over all exposed parts of the person except their mouth and nose, and wrap a vapor barrier—a tent fly, plastic garbage bags, anything that will minimize the escape of heat—around the person.

MUSCLE PULL OR STRAIN

- Apply an ice pack for 20 minutes to any area that hurts. Repeat this every hour until the pain subsides.
- Stretch the sore area gently to rid your body of lactic acid, which contributes to the pain.
- Avoid strenuous activity as long as you're in pain.

POISONOUS PLANT

- Immediately wash everything that might have touched the plant. You may be able to take off the offending oil completely or at least reduce the impending rash.
- Soothe itching with cool, wet compresses.
- Apply lotion containing calamine, alcohol, and zinc acetate; these will dry the blisters and help speed healing.
- Leave a rash open to the air to help it heal.
- Remember that toxic oils from poisonous plants need to be washed out of clothes before wearing them again.

SPRAIN

- Rest the injured limb. Get emergency assistance if you are unable to bear weight on the injured leg, the joint seems unstable or is numb, or you cannot use the joint at all. This may indicate a torn ligament.

- Ice the area. Use a cold pack, a slush bath, or a compression sleeve filled with cold water to help limit swelling after an injury. Try to ice the area as soon as possible after the injury and continue to ice it for 15 to 20 minutes, four to eight times a day, for the first 48 hours or until swelling improves. If you use ice, be careful not to use it too long, as this could cause tissue damage.

- Compress the area with an elastic wrap or bandage. Compression wraps or sleeves made from elastic or neoprene are best.

- Elevate the injured limb above your heart whenever possible to help prevent or limit swelling.

TICK REMOVAL

- Check your naked body from head to toe for ticks—small black, brown, reddish, or tan disklike arachnids (having eight legs) that range from the size of a pinhead to almost the size of a thumbtack. Pay special attention to the backs of your knees, your groin area, and your torso.

- Ask a friend or family member for help if you find a tick in a hard-to-reach spot.

- Hold (or have the other person hold) a pair of tweezers in one hand and grasp the tick with the tweezers close to the surface of your skin. Avoid grabbing the body of the tick with your fingers and trying to pull it out. You might leave some parts of the tick under your skin and also expose your hands to any disease the tick is carrying.

- Gently but firmly pull the tick straight out, working for several seconds if necessary until it loosens and comes free. Occasionally, parts of the tick's mouth become separated from the rest of the tick; if they do, pull them out separately.

- Dispose of the tick by throwing it into a fire, or by squishing it using a tissue and then flushing it down the toilet. Don't smash it with your foot or bare hands.

- Clean the bite site thoroughly with soap and water or Betadine, and thoroughly wash your hands.

LIFESAVING

Lifesaving Skill Essentials

These are skills one needs to have to be able to save someone's life.

- ☐ Bandage a wound
- ☐ Check for signs of life
- ☐ Control bleeding
- ☐ Escape a sinking vehicle
- ☐ Give CPR (cardiopulmonary resuscitation)
- ☐ Help with a severe allergic reaction and use an EpiPen
- ☐ Prevent and treat heatstroke or heat-related events
- ☐ Prevent and treat hypothermia
- ☐ Properly react to and treat a snakebite
- ☐ Safely exit a burning building
- ☐ Save from drowning
- ☐ Treat a burn
- ☐ Treat low blood sugar
- ☐ Treat shock
- ☐ Use aspirin for heart attack or stroke
- ☐ Use the Heimlich maneuver

Lifesaving Skill Extras

- ☐ Use an automated external defibrillator (AED)

To learn first-aid and lifesaving skills from an expert, start with the Red Cross (www.redcross.org/about-us/our-work/training-education.html) or your local Y/YMCA. Outdoor outfitters like L.L. Bean and REI also offer instruction.

ASSEMBLE A DEBRIS HUT

— Find a tree with a low crook.
— Use a sturdy branch as a beam.
— Add smaller sticks.
— Create a roof with leafy branches.
— Insulate the floor with grass, leaves, or pine needles.

TEN ESSENTIALS

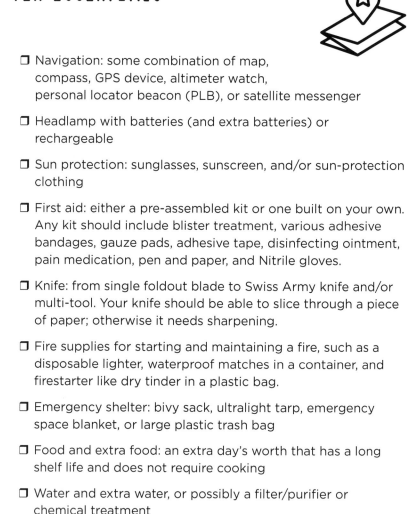

- ❐ Navigation: some combination of map, compass, GPS device, altimeter watch, personal locator beacon (PLB), or satellite messenger

- ❐ Headlamp with batteries (and extra batteries) or rechargeable

- ❐ Sun protection: sunglasses, sunscreen, and/or sun-protection clothing

- ❐ First aid: either a pre-assembled kit or one built on your own. Any kit should include blister treatment, various adhesive bandages, gauze pads, adhesive tape, disinfecting ointment, pain medication, pen and paper, and Nitrile gloves.

- ❐ Knife: from single foldout blade to Swiss Army knife and/or multi-tool. Your knife should be able to slice through a piece of paper; otherwise it needs sharpening.

- ❐ Fire supplies for starting and maintaining a fire, such as a disposable lighter, waterproof matches in a container, and firestarter like dry tinder in a plastic bag.

- ❐ Emergency shelter: bivy sack, ultralight tarp, emergency space blanket, or large plastic trash bag

- ❐ Food and extra food: an extra day's worth that has a long shelf life and does not require cooking

- ❐ Water and extra water, or possibly a filter/purifier or chemical treatment

- ❐ Extra clothes for a change in conditions or what you would need to survive a long, inactive period in the elements

OUTFIT YOURSELF

— Hardware stores carry many of the Ten Essentials.
— Agricultural stores may sell the Ten Essentials.
— Other good sources are outdoor outfitters such as L.L. Bean and REI, which also have retail stores.
— Outdoor essentials, especially camping, can be found at online retailers such as Backcountry, Eddie Bauer, Moosejaw, Patagonia, and many more.
— Local outdoor retailers also offer these items.
— For biking/cycling and water sports, look for local specialty shops or online retailers.

WILDERNESS FIRST AID

Wilderness First-Aid Kit Essentials

- ❏ acetaminophen, ibuprofen, or aspirin
- ❏ adhesive and butterfly bandages, assorted
- ❏ adhesive tape
- ❏ antacid tablets
- ❏ antibiotic ointment
- ❏ antihistamine cream
- ❏ antiseptic ointment
- ❏ antiseptic soap
- ❏ antiseptic towelettes/wet wipes
- ❏ bee-sting kit
- ❏ biodegradable soap
- ❏ blister plasters, moleskin, treatments
- ❏ bulb-irrigating syringe
- ❏ burn ointment, dressing
- ❏ cell phone
- ❏ chemical cold and heat packs
- ❏ cotton balls/cotton swabs
- ❏ diarrhea medicine
- ❏ duct tape
- ❏ elastic wrap/Ace bandage
- ❏ emergency heat-reflecting blanket
- ❏ EpiPens and antihistamine tablets
- ❏ facial-tissue packages
- ❏ first-aid instructions

- ❐ gauze roll and/or pads
- ❐ ground sheet
- ❐ hand sanitizer
- ❐ hydrocortisone cream
- ❐ hydrogen peroxide
- ❐ insect repellent
- ❐ matches
- ❐ medication alert
- ❐ mild laxative
- ❐ mild sedative
- ❐ mirror, small and unbreakable
- ❐ motion-sickness medication
- ❐ paper cups and plastic spoons
- ❐ personal prescription medicines
- ❐ poison-ivy medication
- ❐ razor blade (safety) or knife
- ❐ rubbing alcohol or alcohol swabs
- ❐ safety pins
- ❐ salt tablets or electrolyte powders
- ❐ scissors (blunt tip) or Swiss Army knife with scissors
- ❐ sheet, towels, blanket
- ❐ smelling salts
- ❐ snakebite kit (freeze kit)
- ❐ splints (finger, SAM)
- ❐ sterile gauze pads, two sizes
- ❐ sugar packets and salt packets or rehydration salts
- ❐ sunscreen

- ☐ tourniquet
- ☐ tweezers/tick remover, needle and thread
- ☐ water purification tablets

Wilderness First-Aid Kit Extras

- ☐ compound tincture of benzoin
- ☐ CPR mask
- ☐ First-aid manual
- ☐ hemostatic (blood-stopping) gauze
- ☐ hydrogel-based pads
- ☐ liquid bandage
- ☐ lubricating eye drops
- ☐ medical waste bag
- ☐ notepad and pencil, waterproof
- ☐ sunburn relief
- ☐ thermometer, oral
- ☐ throat lozenges
- ☐ triangular cravat bandage
- ☐ waterproof container for supplies and medications

Wilderness First-Aid Steps

EVALUATION:

- ☐ Size up the scene.
- ☐ Identify life threats.
- ☐ Do a focused exam: head-to-toe check, vital signs, and patient history.
- ☐ Make a problem list and care plan, which includes an evacuation decision.

❑ Treat the patient, providing both medical and emotional support.

❑ Monitor how the patient is doing.

PREPARATION:

❑ Determine whether the area is safe: Ensure no further harm is imminent—for both patient and responders. If a rockslide caused the injury, for example, you might need to move the patient out of the path of additional rockfall.

❑ Identify the mechanism of injury (MOI). Look around to determine what might have caused the accident or injury. That provides clues to the type of injuries that might be present.

❑ Form a general impression of the seriousness of the situation. If the patient is injured, how injured? If the person is sick, how sick?

❑ Determine the number of patients. Don't assume that the most obviously injured person is the only one in need of assessment and care.

❑ Protect yourself: Prudent caregiver practice is to assume all people are infectious. Put on gloves and a mask, and wash hands thoroughly before and after patient contact. (NOLS refers to this as "body substance isolation" [BSI].)

INITIAL PATIENT ASSESSMENT:

❑ Obtain consent to treat (if the person is conscious). Ask the person if you can help. If the answer is "yes," then ask their name, symptoms, and what happened.

❑ Establish responsiveness. Attempt to wake the patient if they aren't responding. (If there is any possibility of a spine injury, you also need to carefully place your hands on either side of the person's head and keep the patient still.)

❑ Airway check: Look in the mouth and check the airway for obstructions.

❑ Breathing check: Look closely at the chest; listen and feel for signs of respiration.

- ❏ Circulation check: Check for a pulse and for major wounds that are bleeding.

- ❏ Disability decision: If you can't rule out a spine injury, continue to protect it.

- ❏ Expose injuries: Without moving the patient, open up clothing covering serious injuries so you can fully evaluate and treat them.

SECONDARY PATIENT ASSESSMENT (HEAD-TO-TOE EXAM):

- ❏ Look: for blood and other bodily fluids, discoloration, or unusual shapes

- ❏ Listen: for airway noises or unusual sounds when joints are moved

- ❏ Feel: for wounds, deformities, and unexpected hardness, softness, or tenderness

- ❏ Smell: for unusual odors

- ❏ Ask: if anything hurts or feels odd or numb

CHECK VITAL SIGNS:

- ❏ Level of responsiveness: Is the patient awake and oriented? Awake and disoriented? Or is your patient unconscious or unresponsive?

- ❏ Heart rate: Using the wrist pulse, check the number of beats per minute and note whether the pulse is strong or weak, regular or irregular.

- ❏ Respiration rate: Check the patient's number of breaths per minute and note whether the breathing is easy or labored.

- ❏ Skin signs: Look at skin color, temperature, and moisture. The inside rim of the lower eye or inside the lower lip are good places to check for color. Is it pink or pale? Is the rest of the skin warm and dry vs. cool and clammy? If possible, also record the patient's temperature with a thermometer.

DO A PATIENT HISTORY:

- ❏ Chief complaint: Ask the following questions: What is your most significant concern? When did it start? What makes it worse or better? Where is it located? How severe is it?

- ❏ How old is the patient?

- ❏ Symptoms: Ask if the patient can provide additional details about the chief complaint, or if they have other conditions or concerns.

- ❏ Allergies: Are there severe ones? (Food and medicine are common ones; also ask about bees.) What are the patient's reactions to their allergies?

- ❏ Medications: Get as many details as possible for both prescription and over-the-counter drugs.

- ❏ Pertinent medical history: Find out if they have any medical conditions that require them to see a doctor for treatment.

LIGHT A FIRE WITHOUT A MATCH

- — Use a flint-and-steel set. You can improvise by using quartzite and the blade of a pocketknife.
- — Use a magnifying glass to focus the sun on a small area with a tinder nest under it.
- — Use another sort of lens (eyeglasses, binocular lens) with the sun.
- — Polish the bottom of a soda can with a chocolate bar (toothpaste also works). Reflect sunlight off the polished can bottom on a focal point and place the tinder about an inch from the point.
- — Use steel wool and a battery (9 volt is best). Stretch out the steel wool to about 6 inches. Rub the battery contacts on the steel wool. Then transfer the burning wool to a tinder nest.

- ❒ Last fluid/food intake, last urine/bowel output: How long ago and how much?
- ❒ Events: Ask if they know what caused the event and the details leading up to it.

TIPS:

- ❒ If possible, have someone of the same gender perform the head-to-toe exam.
- ❒ Have someone help the examiner by writing down observations and vital signs.
- ❒ Assign other tasks, like boiling water for drinks or setting up camp, so that the patient feels like care is orderly and all rescuers have a role.
- ❒ Try to keep the patient clean, warm, and comfortable at all times. If you are waiting for help to arrive, things like shelter, sustenance, and general nursing care will be key to maintaining patient well-being.
- ❒ Fluids are more important than food; avoid caffeinated and sugary drinks.
- ❒ Offer emotional support and empathy.
- ❒ Inform the patient about all aspects of care and involve them in evacuation decisions.
- ❒ Resupply and/or supplement your first-aid kit before each trip (consider a larger tube of antibiotic ointment or more dressing materials, among other things).

WILDERNESS SURVIVAL

You must also have knowledge, mental fitness, and physical fitness for wilderness survival.

Wilderness Survival Kit Essentials

- ❏ aluminum foil
- ❏ batteries and extra batteries for devices
- ❏ biohazard waste bags
- ❏ bow or wire saw
- ❏ canteen
- ❏ cell phone
- ❏ clothing: proper clothing and extra clothing
- ❏ collapsible water jug
- ❏ cordage: nylon rope and parachute cord
- ❏ dental floss, nylon
- ❏ drinking cups
- ❏ duct tape and waterproof tape
- ❏ dust masks
- ❏ emergency bivy
- ❏ emergency/rescue blanket (two-person)
- ❏ facial tissue packages
- ❏ fire: waterproof/windproof matches, lighter, firestarter
- ❏ first-aid kit and personal first-aid kit

- ❏ food procurement items: snare wire, fishing line, fishhooks, fishing tackle
- ❏ hand warmers
- ❏ hand-crank flashlight/radio
- ❏ hydration: water and extra water, water treatment/ purification supplies
- ❏ hygiene kit
- ❏ illumination: flashlight, lanterns, headlamp, emergency candles, light sticks
- ❏ insect repellent
- ❏ insulation: jacket, hat, gloves, rain shell, thermal underwear
- ❏ knife: Swiss Army or other multifunction tool or fixed-blade knife
- ❏ knife sharpener (flint)
- ❏ magnifying glass
- ❏ navigation: topographic map, button compass, orienteering compass, GPS, personal locator beacon
- ❏ needle and thread

- ❏ nutrition: food and extra food
- ❏ personal identification
- ❏ plastic sheet
- ❏ poncho, waterproof
- ❏ pots and skillets
- ❏ repair kit and tools
- ❏ rucksack
- ❏ safety pins
- ❏ safety razor blades
- ❏ shelter: tent, blanket, tarp
- ❏ signal mirror
- ❏ snakebite kit
- ❏ solar/space blanket
- ❏ stove
- ❏ sun protection: sunglasses, sunscreen, hat
- ❏ tarps
- ❏ tools for food handling
- ❏ trash bags
- ❏ trowel, folding
- ❏ waterproof notebook and pencil
- ❏ whistle
- ❏ work gloves
- ❏ ziplock bags

Wilderness Survival Kit Extras

- ❏ axe
- ❏ body warmers
- ❏ canvas, drop cloth, oilcloth, ground pad, thermal blanket
- ❏ emergency water bag

STAY SAFE IN THE WILDERNESS

- — Tell a friend your plans.
- — Dress appropriately.
- — Bring an emergency kit.
- — Monitor weather conditions.
- — Know your route.
- — Be aware of animals.
- — Avoid poisons and venom.
- — Rest and avoid overexertion.

- ☐ flagging tape
- ☐ hammock
- ☐ mule tape
- ☐ pace beads
- ☐ pack baskets
- ☐ sleeping pad
- ☐ solar charger
- ☐ solar lights, fan, generator
- ☐ solar panels or panel kit
- ☐ tinder bundle in sealed bag
- ☐ toilet paper
- ☐ tube tent
- ☐ webbing
- ☐ wool blanket

INDEX

ABOUT THE AUTHOR

Dr. **Barbara Ann Kipfer** is the author of *14,000 Things to Be Happy About* (1.5 million copies in print). She has written seventy other books and calendars, including *Hiking is FUNdamental* and the upcoming *Hiking Ruins in Southern New England,* as well as *Archaeologist's Fieldwork Guide, Encyclopedic Dictionary of Archaeology,* and *1,001 Ways to Live Wild.*

Barbara holds an MPhil and PhD in Linguistics (University of Exeter), a PhD in Archaeology (Greenwich University), an MA and PhD in Buddhist Studies (Akamai University), and a BS in Physical Education (Valparaiso University). She is a Registered Professional Archaeologist, a former sportswriter and editor, and a lexicographer.

Dr. Kipfer worked for companies including Google, Dictionary .com and Thesaurus.com, Answers.com, Ask Jeeves, Zeta Global, General Electric Research, IBM Research, and the *Chicago Tribune*. Her website is www.thingstobehappyabout.com. She lives in Connecticut.